Fallen Angel

Sarah Emambocus

Published by Sarah Emambocus, 2022.

FALLEN ANGEL

First edition. December 31, 2022.

Copyright © 2022 Sarah Emambocus.

ISBN: 979-8201280529

Written by Sarah Emambocus.

Table of Contents

Chapter 1

L ife is full of surprises; you never know what to expect; it is said, *'people come into your life either as a blessing or lesson'*. But I still did not know what fate had planned for me. Our story begins in Madrid, capital of Spain; a city always filled with excitement; in a secluded location at night a man was looking at the city from his study office as he was in thought, *'sometimes, life takes us in places, we never imagined. for me everything started with a dream! the dream to be someone in history! someone people will fear, but most importantly respect! my ambition and determination have made my dream possible! In my world, the night brings the monsters alive. when normal people are asleep, the underground world awakes, and danger is at every corner! I have been through so much, but the best is yet to come!'.*

As there is a knock on the door the person says, *"come in."* A guy enters as he turns to face the Boss. The guy named Liam says, *"Trent I mean sorry Boss"*. Trent has black hair spiky with dark green eyes and a tanned complexion. Trent thinks, *'my story has not always been known to everyone but a few years back I lost my dad Leone who was killed on a mission. I became my own king of the Black Panther Mafia.'* Liam who has blond hair and grey eyes was reading some documents out. Trent was informed of a mission in Amsterdam as Liam asks, *"Boss what do you want to do?"* Trent replies, *"prepare the jet"*. Meanwhile in Germany Amsterdam, a young woman with red hair and brown eyes wearing an apron was working in the kitchen decorating cupcakes. The young

1

woman narrates; *'I am Callie Dawson. Owner of Pretty little Cupcake bakery; life was hard for me as my parents died when I was 6 years old. I spent most of my years at the orphanage however one thing that I always enjoyed doing in school was baking. I never gave up and studied hard achieving a high GPA score for Food Technology and graduating top of my class'.*

As someone comes into the kitchen and says, "*I knew I would find you here Cal*". Callie turns to the person who has long brown curly hair and green eyes. Callie finishes the cupcake as she gives it to her employee to take out. Callie turns to her friend and says, "*Hazel you know work is never finish right?*". Hazel says, *"just come on. we will be late otherwise."* Callie cleaned herself up and removed the apron as they left. As they came to the café they sat down Hazel ordered cocktails and there was a stand-up comedian. Callie looked at Hazel who was enjoying the performance while Callie did not know why but, in her mind, she was reminded of someone familiar. Meanwhile Trent was in his private jet working on some documents on his laptop as he was in deep thoughts over a familiar girl's face. Callie looked at her phone of a younger picture of a guy as she zoomed in and thought, *'Trent Smith a face and name I will never forget.'* Trent opened a folder in his laptop and pulled out a younger picture of a girl as he zoomed in and thought, *'Callie Dawson the Angel and light in my life'.* Both Callie and Trent shared a past.

Soon Hazel noticed Callie was distracted and asks, "*you are not thinking about the guy, right?*". Callie shook her head as she changed what she was looking at. Hazel thought, *'despite us being the best friends I still feel Callie keeps secret from me. but it is ok we all have our secrets and I respect her privacy'.* Hazel's phone rang as she went outside to take the call but soon came back in and told Callie what happened in the bakery who says, "*I think we will need some help.*" Hazel was the PR of the Pretty Little Cupcake bakery and was supporting her best friend grow and promote the business.

Chapter 2

A s Hazel had an idea to help the business; the next day later in the afternoon Callie and Hazel went out to do shopping as Hazel treated Callie to a dress who asked, *"is a new dress really needed?"*. Hazel nods and also buys a new outfit. As the nightfall came, Callie came out from her apartment in the dress which Hazel brought for her; she looked in the mirror to see herself in a short red tight dress while Hazel noticed Callie's hair was tied back in a bun. Hazel said, *"wait a minute."* Hazel takes the clip as Callie's wavy hair comes down. Hazel says, *"much better."* As they leave together Callie is surprised to see she is going to a nightclub and Hazel has VIP access. As they come in Callie sees people dancing and music playing while Hazel goes over to the table and orders champagne. Callie asks, *"Haze what are we doing here?"*. Hazel replies with a smile, *"celebrating"*. As the champagne arrives Hazel hands Callie a glass and clinks in, *'To Pretty little Cupcake'*. They drink and chat when a guy comes over checking Hazel out as saying, *"hey gorgeous want to dance?"*. Hazel did not want to leave Callie however she sensed Hazel's concern and said, *"you should go enjoy Hazel."* Hazel took the guy's hand as he brought her to the dance floor.

Callie finished her drinks a few guys approached and asked her for a dance however she did not really feel like dancing. As she had a few more drinks eventually seeing Hazel with the guy busy she slipped out and called an Uber to take her home. she texted Hazel, *'Enjoy your night and I'll see you tomorrow.'* The next morning Callie came early to the bakery and began baking as usual and checked her schedule. Throughout the day she saw her regular customers and business boomed as always. The next few weeks passed by as soon someone entered the shop wearing a black leather jacket and Black pilot sunglasses. The guy asked, *"can I order a pumpkin spice coffee?"*. Callie prepared and gave it however before telling him how much it was; he simply took it and left. Callie went to the kitchen and saw Hazel busy with the accounts; Callie said, *"we had a customer who didn't pay."* Hazel gets up and says, *"who was he?"*. Callie replies *"I don't know but the guy was kind of strange and he gave me a bad vibe."* Hazel took the rest of the shift that afternoon as she kept an eye out of the guy. As evening came Callie took last shift as a tall guy wearing a suit came into the shop asking, *"hi can I get a French Vanilla frappunico please?"*. Callie prepared it as the guy paid. Callie noticed he had an accent as he asked, *"what's your name?"*. he replied, *"It's Liam."* Liam smiled as he left while Callie thought, *'thank god I don't know what my mind was thinking.'*

As Liam came back to the penthouse, he brought the French Vanilla cappuccino to Trent. Trent was busy with some paperwork on his laptop as he smelled the cappuccino. Trent asked, *"Liam where did you get this?"*. Liam replied, *"from the bakery across town Boss."* Liam asks, *"Boss do you need anything else?"*. Trent shook his head and replied, *"no that will be all."* As Trent was busy on his laptop, he could not help but take a sip of the cappuccino; as he drank it he did not know why but his thought wondered, *'why does this frappunico feel so familiar? The taste of it reminds me of.... Callie. No, it cannot be'*. As he finished the cappuccino he decided to visit the shop tomorrow. Callie closed the bakery and Hazel offered her a ride. Unknown to them someone was watching them in the shadows as Hazel drove Callie home.

As Callie came home, she felt tired, took a shower, and thought about the guy from the bakery, *'he seemed familiar, but I should not worry about it. he was just a customer.'* As Callie looked out from her window at the night sky, she could not help but think of Trent. Callie thought, '*I wonder how Trent is doing. So many years have passed between us.*' Meanwhile Trent finished his work and stared outside at the city and thought of Callie, '*everything I did... I did to protect Callie. I wonder what fate has written for us?*'. They soon both fall asleep while the unknown man who came to Callie's shop enters a private study and says to his Boss, '*I think we might have found Trent's weakness.*' The man says, "*I don't know what source you have received. But keep an eye out and me updated understand.*"

Chapter 3

The next day Trent took Liam to the bakery who asked, *"Boss why are we here?".* Trent replies, *"I am hungry Liam".* As they come into the shop early morning Hazel welcomes them and asks, *"welcome to Pretty Little Cupcakes how can I help you?".* Trent looks around at the treats as its smells delicious and aromatic. Trent asks, *"are you the owner of the bakery?".* Hazel is about to answer just as her mobile rings and says, *"I apologise, Maisie will serve you."* Hazel goes to the back, answers the call to Callie who is at the wholesalers. Hazel says, *"omg! Callie you wouldn't believe there are two hotties."* Callie says, *"focus Hazel. I am missing some items could you just check for me quick?".* Hazel gives the instructions for the remaining products and Callie leaves. Trent orders two French vanilla cappuccino and a pineapple doughnut and jam cupcake. Liam drinks the frappunico and eats the doughnut as he says, *"Yummy this is delicious."* Liam notices Trent is absent-minded and asks, *"Boss are you ok?".* Trent eats the cupcake and drinks the frappunico replying, *"I think we should buy a share into the company."* Liam says, *"Boss you know we are here for a mission."* Trent sighs and thinks, *'I should not get distracted; I must remember why I left Callie. I cannot put her in danger.'*

Meanwhile Callie is driving when suddenly someone comes in front of her as she swerves but hits against a pole. Callie is lightly injured as a small crowd gathers around her. Hazel gets informed of Callie's accident and rushes to the hospital. Callie sees Hazel who asks, *"what happened? Are you ok?".* Callie hugs Hazel as the doctor comes and tells her that it was not serious and to take rest for a few days. Callie comes home and Hazel takes care of her. At the penthouse, Trent was busy with his plans as he wanted to open a company; as he looked online for leases he noticed, *'Pretty little Cupcake'*. He saw an ad for the building next to it and made a call to view for tomorrow. The next day Trent went over to the building which was big and spacious as Trent agreed and paid the fees. Over the next few weeks, he began to develop and enhance the building beside the shop. The unknown guy watched Trent from a distance and gave his report back to his Boss. The Boss was not happy and said, *"we cannot have the Mafia Boss of Black Panther ruling this city."* Callie soon was able to come back to work and noticed the building beside her which had some work done; Callie thought, *'someone must have bought the building'.* Hazel did not know who it was while Callie said, *"maybe we should go and see them."* Hazel says, *"come on Callie I'm sure they will be hosting a party soon."*

A few days later Callie's mind was still curious as she wondered who the owner of the building next door was. Hazel soon came with an invitation to the party next door while Callie said, *"the building must have been done quickly."* Hazel says, *"not really they are turning it into a club called Midnight, but the main party will be held in the penthouse."* Later that evening Hazel came over to help Callie dress up; Callie did not really like to leave her hair down while Hazel said, *"come on Callie who knows you might get noticed?".* Callie thought as she looked in the mirror, *'I do not really want to have anyone else. No guy can ever come close to Trent; I just wish I could see him again.'* Callie asks, *"Haze can you wait for me outside?".* Callie comes to her desk, sees an envelope before thinking of a memory as she reads the letter.

To my love Trent,

Another day passes and I miss you. why are you not back despite the promise you made of your return? I pray you are safe, and I cannot wait to have you back in my arms holding me tight and feeling your warmth. I will make my dream come true soon and I wish you could be by my side.

Never forget me

Yours Callie.

As Callie comes out of her flashback, she puts the letter away and heads out; Hazel and Callie come to the party. The unknown person comes too while Liam recognizes him and alerts Trent. Hazel says, *"maybe there's the two cute guys I saw from the bakery"*. As they come up Trent is in his study as Liam sees Hazel and Callie. Callie says, *"hi Liam"*. Liam says, *"oh hey... um?"*. Hazel says, *"I'm Hazel and this is Callie. She is the owner of Pretty little Cupcakes"*. Liam gets them drinks but then gets a call from Trent; Liam says, *"you should come and meet the owner of Pretty little Cupcakes."* As Hazel needs the toilet; Callie waits as Trent sees Callie's back and says, *"hi you must be the owner of Pretty little Cupcakes"*, Callie had her back turned and thought, *'when I heard his voice that time stood still, and my entire world stopped. I could recognise that voice anywhere... That was Trent's voice... my Trent's voice! The memories of all the moments we have passed together flashed before my eyes.'* Callie takes a deep breath as she turns around and says *"Trent????"*. Trent is stunned and shocked to see Callie and says *"Callie??? How is this possible??? Is that really you?"*. Trent thought so many things in his mind, *'It was Callie! My one and only love here in front of me. I could never forget her brown eyes, She is the most attractive woman on this earth! When I left her, she was a little girl and both of us were kids, but now seeing her here after many years she has grown into a gorgeous woman. I always thought of this moment as I knew this would be both happiest and saddest day of my life.'* Trent notices a sadness in Callie's eyes.

Chapter 4

T rent was stunned and surprised to see Callie and said, *"you're the manager of Pretty Little Cupcake."* Callie was too stunned and surprised to see him as she remembered Hazel telling her about the rich owner who has just moved in next door; as Callie asks, *"Trent please don't tell me you are the one who bought the building next door!".* Trent replies," *yes the building next door is my nightclub!".* Callie felt anger in her and thought, *'what??? What is he trying to do? What game is he playing at?'.* Callie feels annoyed as she heads out while Trent thinks as he watches her leave, *'did she just walked away from me after seeing me for the first time in years? Oh, no, Callie! If fate wants us as one, I will not wreck this chance for anything in the world!'.* As Trent goes after Callie; the unknown man (Vyom) who has been watching the scene calls his Boss and informs him, *"Trent has gone after Callie, she must be very special to him."* His Boss replies *"report back to the base and we will plan what to do next."* Vyom leaves as Hazel comes back to the party and searches for Callie; she wonders, *'where did Callie disappear to?'.* Callie had come downstairs into the reception as she sat by the window looking outside while Trent came downstairs looking for her and saw her by the window. Callie and Trent's eyes lock as he came closer to her.

Callie thought as she looked at Trent, *'I still cannot believe he is here, somehow I prayed that everything was a dream; knowing Trent was next door to me was not going to be easy. no matter how heartbroken I was when he abandoned me; my heart was still madly in love with him. but I need to stay strong and cannot let him escape without knowing why he did leave me all those years ago.'* Callie looked angrily at Trent as he called her *'Angel'* as she replied, *"Angel??? I am not your Angel Trent? Why did you have to come back? Why here? why now?"*. Trent replied, *"honestly Callie, I didn't know you were the owner of Pretty Little Cupcake; I may have had a feeling, but I never expected to see you again."* As Trent comes closer to Callie, he holds her closer as they stare into each other's eyes as he asks, *"do you want me to leave? After being away from you all these years, is that how much you despise me?"*. Callie response coldly to Trent *"what do you think Trent? A love confession? You broke my heart and left me all alone, our relationship and all the promises broken!"*. Trent says, *"I love you always and still do Angel."* Callie laughs and says, *"did you always believe that I would wait for you? I have my life at the bakery, and you are not part of it."* He says, *"I can change it! do you think for one moment now that I will let you leave! I want one chance; I will justify to you everything and if you want then you can punish me."* As he pulls her closer; Liam comes and interrupts them as he says, *"Boss."* Trent let Callie go as he looked at Liam with a cold stare as Callie thought, *'why is Liam calling you Boss? What are you hiding?'*. Callie felt uneasy, called an Uber, and went home.

As Liam and Trent talked; Trent told Liam how much Callie meant to him whilst Callie came home Trent asked, *"Liam I want you to get all the information on Callie."* Trent looked around to find Callie however he could not find her and headed back upstairs to the party; he saw Hazel and asks, *"have you seen Callie?"*. Callie phoned Hazel as she picked up; *"hey Callie where are you?"*; Callie replies *"I was not feeling too well and took an Uber home. come soon."* Hazel ended the call and told Trent Callie was at home; Trent asked, *"Hazel can I please have Callie's number?"*. Hazel was surprised and thought, *'wow a guy actually taking an interest in Callie.'* Hazel gave Trent Callie's number as he saved it on his mobile; as Hazel says, *"I might as well tell you all this as you are the first guy to notice Callie. She has never dated or been with anyone else."* Hazel leaves just as Trent had a smile on his face after hearing Hazel's words and thought, *'finding out Callie has not dated or been with anyone filled me with joy. She was one of a kind and I loved my Angel'.* Hazel comes to Callie's place as she was eating ice-cream and watching *'You'* on Netflix; Hazel removes her heels and says, *"Mr. hotness was asking about you."* Callie replies, *"excuse me? who?".* Hazel mentions Trent while Callie sighs and says, *"Haze I think it's time I told you about my childhood lover from the photo."* Hazel says *"wait is this your biggest secret? The one you never told me about?".* Callie nods as she sits on the couch; Callie switches off the TV and is about to tell Hazel her story. Back in a secluded location Vyom is with his Boss with information on Callie as the Boss says in a sinister voice; *'we will order a hitman to get rid of Callie, once Trent is broken; he will be easy to attack to bring down.'*

Chapter 5

Back at Callie's apartment, she was sitting with Hazel who was waiting for Callie to tell her the story; Callie narrates her childhood.

'Years ago, I was raised in St George's orphanage in Italy or also known as 'Hell'. I never knew my parents as the warden had told me they died when I was six years old; The Warden was extremely strict and often made me and all the kids to work and clean everywhere. Soon a new boy came, and his name was Trent Smith; he had black curly hair and green eyes. He developed a friendship with me, and we both become close like planning our future together. However, when we had attempted to make an escape, I sprained my arm whilst I told Trent to leave as he promised to come back to save me, but he never did. (End of flashback)

As Callie sighs drinking the tea, Hazel says, *"I can't believe Trent abandoned you. you loved him for so many years."* Callie replies, *"he's still my first love. I've never dated anyone else and now you know why."* Hazel asks, *"now that he's back will you give him a chance?"* Callie was in thoughts over this; meanwhile back at Trent's penthouse he was still thinking about Callie; as Liam came there, he said, *"Boss."* He hands a file to Trent who opens to find information Callie. Trent says, *"Liam I want you to hide Callie's identity; everything from our childhood and family."* Trent thought, *'I have a lot of enemies and if anyone finds out about Callie's relationship to me it will make her a target and put her at risk.'* Trent looks at Liam and says, *"Liam I want you to understand*

Callie is more important to me than my own life! if you have to choose between my life and Callie's in any position, you need to choose her always!". Liam is stunned as he says, *"Boss, this isn't how it works! I swore my loyalty to you and protect you with my life!".* As Trent clears the discussion with Liam; he then asks, *"who did you send over to keep an eye on Callie's place?".* Liam replies, *"Boss I have sent over Mason and Elijah".*

At Callie's apartment Hazel was watching the *'squid game'*. As Hazel mentions to Callie, *"did I tell you that Trent looks like a hot and dangerous Mafia boss?".* Callie had a serious expression her face and replies, *"if he has anything to do with the Mafia, he better return wherever he came from!".* Just then a glass is smashed from the bedroom. Callie says, *"Haze, go hide and lock yourself in the bathroom."* Hazel was worried as she asks, *"what about you Callie? I am not going to leave you alone."* Callie replies, *"I will be fine!".* Callie comes to the bedroom; she sees the glass pieces shattered on the floor as the unknown guy is pointing a gun at her. Callie angrily says, *"who the hell do you think you are? Breaking in here?".* The man tells her, *"SHUT UP! I am the only one to ask you questions; how are you connected to the Black Panther Mafia leader?".* Callie was stunned, surprised and shocked as she replies, *"I have no clue what you are talking about! Who or what is the Black Panther Mafia? I have no knowledge or anything to do with the Mafia world."* Callie thought for a moment as she put the pieces like a puzzle in her mind as her expression from fear turned into anger and she thought, *'Trent? How could he come back to my life like this! he is a fucking Mafia Boss!".* Before Callie could do anything, a gunshot was fired.

Chapter 6

As Callie opened her eyes, she saw someone had come to her side and was beating the man up. Mason says, *"wait until my Boss handles you!"* As Callie watched seeing the bloodshed and fighting; she did not know how what to think. Callie notices the unknown man lying on the floor as she asks nervously, *"um.. is he dead?".* Mason replies, *"no it is something done by my boss! are you ok? Did he do anything to you?".* Callie felt anger in her eyes saying, *"what the hell! You are asking me how am I? I have just watched someone getting shot and this was in front of me and not on a motion picture screen! Call your Boss right now and pass me the phone!".* Back at Trent's penthouse he saw Mason call as he answers, however was stunned to hear who was on the phone; Callie says angrily, *"I want you to take your lap dog and your damn self far away from me Trent, or should I address you as Boss of the Black Panther?".* Trent was stunned as he asked questions, *"Angel? What happened? Is everything ok? How do you know who I am?".* As Callie felt frustrated and anger, she says to Trent, *" stay away from me."* Callie disconnects the phone and hands it back to Mason.

As Mason brings Callie to the living room. Callie remembers Hazel as she opens the bathroom to find it empty as she looks at Mason and says, *"what have you done to my best friend?".* Mason replies *"she is ok and was taken home."* Callie sighs, sits on the sofa and tries to get Mason to leave. A few moments later Trent knocked on the door as Callie opened to see Trent holding a gun in his hand and wanting to know what happened. Mason went outside while Callie was still in shock. Trent sighs and says, *"I should have explained everything at the party?"*. Callie rolls her eyes and says, *"what were you supposed to tell me? that the boy I grew up is gone and standing in front of me right now is a Mafia Boss?"*. Trent says, *"Angel you didn't give me a chance to explain properly?"*. Callie points angrily at Trent as she says, *"A chance??? Do you know how many times I thought of your return? How many times I wanted to forgive and forget everything only for you to come back?"*. Trent pleads in front of Callie as he says, *"forgive me for being away from you for all these years; let's start over."* Callie says, *"and what do you want? for me to become a girlfriend of a monster or mob boss?"*. As Callie talks about her life, Trent steps in and says, *"Angel, your life is more precious than mine"*. Callie asks; *"then why Trent, why have you come back now?"*.

Trent says, *"I never knew you were here! Protecting you is the only reason I did not come back or looked for you all these years. Do you think it did not kill and hurt me inside everyday not knowing how you are?"* Callie asks; *"then why instead of becoming a Mafia Boss, you did not come back for me like you promised!"*. Trent says angrily; *"how about you listen to me before you jump to conclusions? It is easy to stand there and point the finger at me when you have no idea what I have been through all these years!"* Callie takes a deep breath and says, *"then tell me! tell me why you never came back! But if you do not prove to me for any reason, I want you to promise me you will leave here and never come back!"*. Trent looks at Callie says, *"if after you hear me out, you want me out of your life, then so be it!"*.

Chapter 7

Trent says firmly, "*Callie you need to come with me.*" Callie coldly replies, *"I won't come with you."* Trent sighs and says calmly, "*Callie please just pack a bag and come otherwise you will be in danger, and I cannot allow that"*. Callie heads to her room and comes back carrying a small bag with her. As they head out Trent and Callie drive to his penthouse; soon they come in Callie says, *"I am tired where is the room?"*. As Trent calls Liam, he comes out asking, *"Boss what is it?"*. Liam sees Callie and says surprised, *"Callie."* Trent gives Liam a cold stare and says, "*show Callie to her room.*" Liam takes Callie down the corridor as she opens the door. Callie heads in as she closes the door; Liam comes back to Trent who says, *"you will address her as Miss Callie from now on."* Liam nods as Callie thought; *'why was I feeling sad and worried thinking Trent may leave again and never come back! Damn my stupid heart giving me mixed emotions. I guess I will have to hear his story tomorrow'*. Callie soon fell asleep; the next morning Callie awoke early as she has a phone call from Hazel. Callie asks, *"can you manage the bakery today?"*. Hazel replies, *"of course I can Callie; We need to speak later though about you know."*

Callie hangs up as she changes out of her pjs. Trent is in the living room drinking as Callie comes to the living room as Trent sees her; Trent stops drinking as he says, *"did you sleep well? you must be hungry."* Trent prepares egg, bacon and toast as Callie says surprised, *"you can cook now."* Trent says, " *yep I can cook pasta and breakfast."* Callie smiles however she says, "*Trent I want to hear what happened and how you became the Mafia boss.*" Trent sighs as he narrates; '*the day I left you 20 years ago was the worst day of my life...*

A flashback memory shows back to night Trent ran away and escaped from the orphanage in Italy; 'I ran as fast as I could until I got in one of those streets neither the rats do not want to be on! I was very scared and suddenly I heard two guys talking under a lamppost. There were two guys talking on the street as one of them yelled, "*we need someone to do this job.*" As they saw me, I was called over as I crossed the road and they asked about what I was doing there; I needed money to save you and I explained that I had run away from the orphanage. one gave me instructions and I ran in the opposite direction. As I went another guy came in a leather jacket yelling "*what are you fuckers doing? Why are you not making money?*" right now, you are not only wasting your time but my time too!*" one of them said "*your money will be with you soon. we have sent someone to get it*'.

Chapter 8

As Trent ran back, he was hurt and crying as he apologised for not being able to get the money. The man in leather jacket was shocked as he brought his gun out and shot the two men. As Trent pleaded for his life he says, *"please don't kill me! I tried to do the job; I need to save my Angel"*. Alex says, *"I heard that they said you have no family."* Trent nods as Alex says, *"come with me."* As Trent left with Alex; they flew to Spain; Alex brought him into a fancy mansion. Trent waits outside as Alex goes into the office and informs the boss of what happened; Alex soon calls Trent to come inside. He says, *"Trent meet my boss the leader of the Black Panther Mafia."* Trent was worried as the man looks at Trent and says, *"Alex please leave us."* Trent was scared while the man says, *"do not worry I will not harm you son. My name is Leone Reeves."* Trent says, *"it's a pleasure to meet you sir."* Leone says, *"I have only one question to ask you. what would you sacrifice to protect your family?"* Trent replies, *"I would give up my own life sir."* Leone welcomes Trent into the family.

Time passed as eight years changed so much in Trent's life as he trained and became stronger under Leone's training and command. I never stopped thinking of you my Angel while Leone become more stricter with me and says, *"the girl will be your weakness."* Trent says, *"she is not my weakness but my strength"*. Ten years changed on the night of my 21st birthday as Leone decided to give me my gift for which I had longed! After a meeting in Spain that evening, Leone decided to come with me to Italy and bring you with us. However, the helicopter we were in crashed and everything changed in a second. As we landed in the woods, I got up and looked for Leone who was severely injured. I held his head on my lap trying to help him, but the blood and his wounds were very deep. Leone says, *"Trent you are the son I never had, and I am grateful for Alex bringing you to me."* Trent says, *"You are the father I always wished for."* Leone gives Trent a few more words and advises him, *"I know you love Callie very much, but you know becoming the leader of the Black Panther Mafia means danger. Will you be able to protect her?".* Trent had tears in his eyes as Leone says, *"I will always be with you son watching over you."* As it heavily rains Trent cries holding Leone who says, *"that day my name changed forever; becoming Trent Reeves not just meant power but respect."* (End of flashback)

As Trent wiped a tear from his eyes, he looks at Callie and says, *"the day that Leone died in my arms, my heart died and went with him, and from that day I made the choice to be away from you! my enemies and death follows me."* Callie looked at Trent sadly who says, *"if you want me to leave now I will. Is my life story not enough for you to understand me or forgive me? have I lost my chance to become yours?"*

Chapter 9

After Callie heard Trent's story of what happened years ago; she felt his pain as Callie says, *"Trent this is a lot to take in."* As Trent holds her hand saying, *I do not expect you to pretend to forget everything right now. I only want to be able to win you back. It was a mistake to stay away from you, but I did nothing else than to protect you."* Callie looks at him saying, *"I don't know if being away from you is the best for me! you decided all those years to leave me."* Trent says, *"I did a mistake doing that. Let us start over! We have been in love with each other since we were kids. We cannot deny we are made for each other."* Callie says, *"I have to get to work."* As Callie leaves Trent thinks, *'my Angel I will win you back.'* In the bakery it was busy as Hazel was trying to manage everything when Callie came and said, *"hey".* Hazel says, *"you have finally come Calls."* Callie kept herself busy with the baking and serving the customers however she knew she had to decide about Trent. Elsewhere, Trent came to the nightclub as he was doing some deals however Liam went next door as Callie says, *"hi Liam."* Liam asks, *"hey, can I order the usual?"* Callie serves him and Liam pays before leaving. As the evening approaches Callie closes up the bakery as she sees the nightclub next door; she thinks about the broken window at her place; *'how am I supposed to go home?'.* Just as Callie walks down the road, she sees Trent waiting for her. Trent says, *"I know your place is still waiting to be fix. You can stay with me."* Callie smiles and nods at him.

As they walk home; Callie looks at Trent as she remembers a small memory in the orphanage; one evening Callie got ill with a high fever whilst doing the washing and Trent came and stayed by her side; Trent let Callie wear his jumper as she cuddled in his arms. Callie asked, *"do you ever think of your life outside of here?"* Trent replies; *"of course, I do, every day and night."* Callie asks; *"what do you see?"* Trent replies: *"I see us living in an incredible penthouse."* Callie says, *"with a big kitchen ? You know how much I love to bake".* Trent nods and says, *"yes, and a big kitchen! Also, with a beautiful garden".* Callie asks; *"and what about ice-cream and treats?"* Trent says, *"of course my angel, for you I will do anything!".* Trent sees Callie asleep as he kisses her forehead and soon sleep as well. (End of memory flashback)

As they stop; Trent sees Callie and asks, *"are you ok?".* Callie looks at Trent and says, *"would you like to get some ice-cream?".* Trent says, *"sure".* They come to a nearby ice-cream stall as Trent says, *"can I get one Vanilla and raspberry ripple and one chocolate rocky road please?".* Trent pays as they enjoy the ice-cream. Meanwhile an unknown person is watching Callie and Trent as they capture some photos. Callie and Trent head back as Callie says, *"Trent I think we should do something tomorrow."* Trent asks, *"what do you mean like a date?".* Callie nods as she heads to her room to sleep while Trent has a smile on his face. The unknown man brings photos of Callie and Trent as the man smirks and asks, *"will you be ready for tomorrow?".* Vyom nods and says, *"yes Boss."*

Chapter 10

The next day Callie comes to the bakery as she bakes some cakes and biscuits as Hazel asks, *"is everything ok?"*. As they talk; meanwhile Liam comes to Trent in the office as he says, *" Boss I have something to tell you, the prime minster of Italy has been interfering with our business and shipments on the docks."* Trent says, *"what?"*. As Liam explains about the deals and business which could get affected in Italy; Trent says, *"I guess we better go and meet the prime minster; prepare the jet."* Liam nods as they leave as they head for the flight to Sicily; Liam explains in more details to Trent as he says, *"don't worry I will sort the situation out."*

As Trent soon lands in Sicily, he goes to see the Prime Minister as Sabrina is inside her office as Nate says, *"Madam what you are planning is a big mistake"* . Sabrina says, *"I am aware of what I am doing."* As Nate tries to stop her asking, *"do they have any information that could blackmail or put you in danger?"*. Sabrina replies, *"no but what we are doing is top secret and no one must know"*. Sabrina thinks, *'Trent Reeves is the only one that can help me with this job.'* Nate gets a message through his earpiece and informs Sabrina as she gives permission for Trent to enter. Trent comes in as Nate leaves waiting outside as Trent looks around and then at Sabrina. He thinks, *'why does she look so familiar? Have I seen her before?'*. Trent says, *"Miss Prime Minister it's an honour to meet you, when my men Liam informed me, you were messing with my shipments I felt worried however I am calm as you see."* Sabrina rolls her eyes as she says, *"you can drop the act Trent Reeves."* Trent questions Sabrina's intention of meddling in his work as Sabrina says, *"I am here to make a deal with you regarding an urgent matter."* Trent laughs as he was stunned and says, *"what could a Prime minister want or offer from me? can I call you Sabrina, as I think we will become good friends.".* Sabrina looks at him as Trent gives her money however Sabrina snaps and says, *"I don't need your corrupt money! If I choose to, I could bring down all your operations and businesses, but I will not".* Trent looks at her with anger while Sabrina takes a deep breath and says, *"Trent, I would like you to help me find someone."* Trent was surprised as Sabrina told him her family background. Trent agreed and said, *"give me a name and pictures and your job will done."* Sabrina says, *"that's the problem, I don't have any pictures! This is something I have kept secret for years! My husband died a few years back, but we had a daughter 20 years ago! She was kidnapped from the front of my house and since then there has been no trace of her, I do not even know if she is alive or..."* After hearing everything, Sabrina takes a tissue and says, *"I made it my life objective to finding Sophia and even becoming the Prime Minister with power I was unable to find anything which is why I believe you are my only chance of finding her."* Trent agrees to help her as he says, *"Sabrina, I give you my word, but this needs to be secret and quiet."* Sabrina nods, extends her hand as Trent shakes it. As they discuss a few more things; Trent soon comes out of the office.

Liam asks, *"Boss how did it go?".* Trent replies, *"I'll tell you in the jet."* As they head to the jet Liam is stunned to hear from Trent about the Prime Minister having a daughter. Trent thinks, *'the girl has Callie's age'.* Liam asks, *"Boss do you think the girl is alive?".* Trent is not sure how to answer the question buts gives Liam a small reply, *"I don't know Liam we are talking 20 years back and if the Italian Cartels are behind this then."* As they soon head back to Amsterdam, Trent thinks of Callie. As evening falls over the city Callie locks up the bakery, checks her phone as she waits for Trent; a few hours pass as Callie thinks, *'has Trent stood me up? has he given up on me?'.*

Chapter 11

As Callie waited and thought, *'I know yesterday we agreed to have a date, but my mind was feeling uncertain, and I was feeling conflicted.'* Hazel sees Callie outside and offers her a ride however Callie tells Hazel she was waiting for Trent. Hazel says, *"I'll see you tomorrow"* Callie worries as she does not have Trent's number; she checks the time and sees it is late and begins to walk; an unknown man sees her and says, *"look at this delicious babe!"*. As the guy approaches Callie, he tries to touch her however Callie slaps him and says, *"don't you dare touch me you dickhead!"*. As she has her phone in her hand, she threatens to call the police; the unknown man kicks her and forces her to take a drug as Callie thinks, *'everything is coming blurry. Trent where are you?'*. As the unknown man tries to drag her away; Trent sees what is happening as he cocks his gun as Callie opens her eyes briefly to see Trent before a gunshot is fired.

The man tries to take her as Trent sees Callie's state and yells, *"GET AWAY FROM HER BASTARD!"*. As Trent cocks his gun so does the unknown guy as Callie opens her eyes and sees Trent however soon everything goes black, and the last thing Callie hears is a gunshot fired. A few hours later Trent is with the doctor in his room as Callie is on the bed. Trent asks, *"how is she doing?"*. The doctor tries to calm him down however Trent angrily says, *"JUST TELL ME HOW IS SHE?!"*. The doctor informs and assures Trent, *"Callie is fine, she needs rest and also her blood level was low most likely because she hasn't been eating properly."* Trent calms down as he drops the doctor to the door. Liam asks, *"Boss how is Callie?".* Trent informs Liam what the doctor had told him as he gives Liam instructions to watch Callie. As Trent heads down to the basement below he was fighting the unknown man who had hurt Callie. Trent angrily punches him and says, *"no one touches my Angel and lives to see another day."* As the man pleads for his life to be ended, Trent beats him up badly; back in Trent's room Callie stirs from her sleep as she remembers what happened earlier with Trent and the unknown man. Callie opens her eyes looking around and then remembering the gunshot; she runs out screaming Trent's name. Liam hears Callie's voice who asks, *"Liam how is Trent? Where is he? Is he ok?".* Liam assures Callie that Trent is fine as Callie cries and confesses how much she loves Trent. Liam says, *"I know how you must be feeling, and you will become strong Callie."* Callie replies, *"I don't know if I can be part of this dangerous life!".* As Liam tells Callie about the unknown's guy business such as raping woman and human trafficking ; Callie feels anger boiling as she says, *"Liam can you get me a glass of water?".* Liam nods as he turns, and Callie grabs his gun from his pocket. Callie head to the lower level to find Trent. As Trent is beating the guy to the point where he can no longer stand; Trent cocks his gun however as a gunshot is fired.

Trent looked around as he saw Callie holding a gun. Trent came to Callie and said, *"what are you doing here Angel?".* Trent felt anger and says, *"you shouldn't have shot him! You are an Angel, and Angels never get their hands dirty with blood! ! Look at me! I am the devil here, and you are the Angel!".* Callie drops the gun and is angry and says, *"Trent the world isn't what we had imagined it to be, and I can't be an Angel whilst seeing innocent people killed or murdered every day."* Trent uses his commanding voice and says, *"I AM THE BOSS AND I MAKE THE DECSIONS!".* Callie slaps Trent and says, *"don't you dare raise your voice at me!".* Callie leaves as Trent sighs and thinks, *'why did I have to yell at her?'.*

Chapter 12

A s Callie came back into the room in tears thinking about what she had just done. Trent comes to the door as he says, *"Angel, please don't cry! Each one of your tears is just like a knife stabbing me in the heart!"* Callie says, *"leave me alone, I want to be by myself."* Trent says, *"I know what you are feeling right now! I can never forget the first time I had to kill someone."* Callie opens the door as she asks, *"how did you feel when you killed someone for the first time?"*. Trent tells her what happened and says, *"I wasn't as strong as you are just now."* Meanwhile in the Boss's hideout, Vyom informed him that Trent had killed the men; As the Boss had an angry look in his eyes, he gave Vyom an instruction; back in the penthouse Callie and Trent sorted things as Callie apologises for slapping Trent. As Trent pulls her in, they share a kiss while Callie says, *"Trent I have something you need to know"*. Trent's phone rings as he goes into the other room. Callie looks at the time and says, *"I will give Hazel a call."* As they talk; Hazel invites Callie to the party and she says, *"I will get changed and send me the location."* As Hazel drinks and looks around, she soon grabs the attention of a young guy as he comes over and introduces himself as Oliver. Hazel flirts with Oliver however as Oliver gets a notification on his phone. Hazel wonders, *'has he got a girlfriend or something?'*. Oliver says, *"I will be in a few minutes babes."* Oliver leaves as Hazel gets Callie's call and says, *"I am nearby."*

Meanwhile Oliver was outside as he came to see a man smoking as he says, *"finally you have come. I was worried I wouldn't see you."* As they both start talking; Oliver says, "*come and have a drink with me bro, I just met the most remarkable young lady.*" Oliver warns him not to take his girl as they head upstairs to the party in the sky rooftop. Callie tells Hazel all about her kiss but does not mention the Mafia stuff and shooting. Hazel asks, "*have you told Trent about your secret?*". Callie replies "*not yet but Hazel being with Trent will change everything.*" As Hazel gives Callie relationship and dating advice; Oliver comes back as Hazel says, "*Ollie you came back; let me introduce you to my best friend and sister Callie.*" Oliver shakes Callie's hand as Hazel smiles at Oliver however Hazel and Callie see a guy next to Oliver who looks handsome and mysterious; Oliver says, "*allow me to introduce my older brother Holden.*" Storm looks at Callie and thinks, '*wow she is sexy*'.

Chapter 13

Storm says, *"Nice to meet both of you.".* As Hazel flirts with Storm and tries to matchmake her friend Callie with him. Callie is embarrassed and heads over to the bar. Oliver feels sad and hurt as Callie thinks of Storm. Storm comes over and says, *"Callie, I think you are a lovely woman."* As Hazel notices the pain in Oliver's face; Oliver says, *"you like my brother, don't you?".* As Oliver explains how he is feeling and also confesses, *'I like you Haze.'* Hazel is stunned as she comes over and says, *"I feel what you are feeling because, Callie is hotter than me and she gets all the guys."* As Oliver turns to leave; Hazel holds his hand, pulls him to her and kisses him. They both kiss each other with passion as Oliver asks, *" should we continue this at my place or yours?".* Hazel takes his hand and says, *"mine let's go."* As they leave; Callie is drinking at the bar while Storm tries to flirt with her. Storm asks, *"do you have a boyfriend?".* Callie gives mixed response as Storm holds Callie's waist and says, *"Callie you must not that I am not a good guy, and you deserve better. But for some reason you are special, and I know that if we ever meet again, I want to win your heart."* As Storm leaves leaving Callie in deep thoughts; she checks her phone as it is really late and heads back to Trent's place. In the living room Trent is worried as he looks at the time wondering, *'where could she be?'.* As Callie rings the bell; Trent opens and sees Callie is tired and drunk. As Trent questions her, *"where were you Angel?".* Callie yawns and replies, *"I was with Hazel'.*

As Trent tries to explain how worried and dangerous it is for Callie to be out alone. Callie feels anger and says, *"you are responsible for all this, bringing danger and coming back. What do you expect me to do? Be like an Angel for you trapped in a silver cage?"*. Callie says, *"I'd rather stay at my place right now and get this straight Trent, if you want us to work then don't command or control me!"*. Callie calls an Uber and heads home while Trent calls his men to watch Callie's apartment. As he ends the call, he sees another incoming call from a private number as he answers *"hello? who is this?"*. Sabrina replies, *"Trent it's Sabrina here, The prime minister of Italy."* Sabrina informs him that the number she is calling from will be used to communicate. Trent says, *"Sabrina I was awaiting for more information from you so that I can begin the job and send my men out."* Sabrina was annoyed and said firmly, *"I have sent all the documentation to you which should arrive by tomorrow morning! I want you to be in charge of this job Trent. This is the deal we have."* As Trent assures Sabrina he hangs up thinking, *'the sooner her daughter is found, the sooner she will be off my case.'* Meanwhile at the base Vyom comes in and says, *"Boss he has arrived."* As Vyom has some doubts, the Boss says, *"he is the best man to do this job; now tell Storm to come in."* As Storm comes in, he asks, *"what can I do for you?"*. Seth says, *"I need you to do a job! You are the only person that can get rid of this person for me."* Seth puts forward an envelope in front of him.

Chapter 14

A s Storm takes the envelope and is about to open it; he puts it down as Seth looks at him and says, *"I'm not giving you a choice Storm! You are here and you will work for me!"*. Storm says, *"listen to me, you called me to offer me a job and I have not agreed yet! But let me be clear! I am Storm and I don't work for anyone by myself!"*. Seth *thinks, 'you bastard! As soon as you have done this job you will be dead next!'*. Seth tries to calm him down and explain about money whilst Storm says, *"I work with you to get the job done for my money, tell me who do you wish to kill?"*. Seth replies *"Callie Dawson,"*. As Storm is about to open the envelope he thinks for a moment while Seth asks, *"will you be able to take the job?"*

As Seth mentions how important Callie is to Trent Reeves. Storm sorts out everything he soon leaves with the envelope. Seth calls in Vyom saying, *"after the mission is done; order the men to get rid of Storm."* Vyom says *"but Boss you know he is the best hitman."* Seth rolls his eyes; The next morning Callie awakes with a hangover; she remembers the fight with Trent and also meeting Holden; as she freshens up; the doorbell rings, Callie opens to find Trent at the door. Trent comes in as she asks, *"what are you doing here?* Trent smiles seeing her; as he comes closer to her as Trent says, *"something I want to be doing for the rest of my life, Callie. I cannot explain to you in words how much I love you. I want to be patient, win you over, and have you trusting me Angel, but I do not know how long I will be able to hold myself. I love you Callie and I want you so fucking bad that I cannot breathe or think straight!"*

They both kiss passionately as she says, "*we should stop this!*" Trent says, "*please don't ask me to stop Callie. I have been dreaming about this moment for years. I want to make you mine!* " Callie is nervous whilst Trent asks for a chance for their relationship, "*Angel will you be mine? Will you be my girlfriend?*". Callie was stunned and surprised by Trent's question as she nods. As they sort things out between them Callie was happy to be with Trent officially however Trent was even more happy as Callie was not just his first kiss, but he would also be her first everything. Meanwhile in Hazel's apartment she was kissing Oliver as the doorbell rang as Hazel tried to ignore it. She eventually opened the door and was stunned to see Storm. Hazel asks, "*Holden what are you doing here?*". Storm comes in holding the envelope as he opens it and sees Callie's photo; Hazel gets dressed as Oliver asks, "*Bro what are you doing here?*". Storm replies, "*I need Hazel to find your friend Callie!*"

Chapter 15

Hazel asks, *"what is your concern with her? Holden Callie's is not any type of girl, she is...."* Storm says, *"she's extraordinary I know! I do not want to take a lot of your time, as I can see you are busy! All I am asking is to know her address! I need to talk to her!".* Hazel says, *"ok fine, I will tell you her work address, but only as I want you to leave."* Later on, that same day in Callie's bakery she hears a knock on the door as she says; *"come on in!"* Callie is stunned to see who it is and says, *"you????? what are you doing here????"* Storm comes in and says, *"nice to see you too, Callie!".* Callie says, *"Holden, you made it very clear last night that you are not going to come after me".* Storm says, *"things changed! I am here because I want to speak with you".* Callie says, *"you don't know me! what can you want to talk to me about?"* Storm says, *"yes, you are right! I do not know you, but I would love to get to know you, Callie!"* He comes closer to her as Callie says, *"Holden, this is not right!"* Storm asks; *"what is not right? I am not touching you! or would you like me to do it?"* Callie says, *"you are too close to me!"* Holden asks; *"and is this something bad?"* Callie's phone rings as she says, *"that is my phone! I have to get that!"*

Storm steps back as Callie answers her phone; *"Trent???? Is everything all right?"* Storm is shocked at his realisation that Callie is the same one he has been ordered to kill. *Callie says, "ok then! I will wait for you here! See you later!"* As she ends the call Storm asks; *"was that Trent Reeves?".* Storm waits for a response as Callie is stunned and asks; *"how do you know Trent?"* Storm asks, *"Callie, are you the woman*

33

of Trent Reeves?" Callie pauses for a moment as she says, *"of course you know Trent, because you are part of the same world, aren't you???"* Storm is in a deep thought; as Callie says angrily; *"answer me, damnit!"* Storm says, *"yes I am part of the same world as Trent Reeves!"* Callie comes up to him, punches him and asks, *"did you get close to me so that you can hurt Trent??"* Storm replies angrily; *"don't you dare to raise your hand on me again, Callie! You do not know who you are messing with!"*. Callie says, *"I could say the same! Stay away from me before this end badly, ok??? "* Storm says, *"with pleasure!"*. Meanwhile Trent was in his nightclub office working on Sabrina's case while Liam also assisting says, *"all this show boss is that the person who took the prime minister's daughter is still alive."* As they talk more about the case, Trent asks Liam to get a location as he goes to the computer and has a look until he find something. Liam calls Trent over as Trent says, *"we have to go back to Italy!"*. As Liam asks, *"Boss do you want me to prepare everything for our flight?"*.

Trent replies, *"not yet."* Trent tells Liam about Callie giving him a chance while Liam is happy for Trent however Liam also in worried about the case of the girl. Meanwhile an unknown girl gets a text and gets on a flight to Amsterdam. As Callie finishes the afternoon shift at the bakery, Hazel comes to the office; Callie tells Hazel everything. Hazel: says, *"I can't believe he would try to use you and Trent."* Callie asks, *"why did you even send him here in the first place?"*. Hazel replies, *"I thought by the way he was looking at you that he..."*. Just then a voice interrupts them as Trent says, *"who was looking at you Angel? Hazel, can you give me a minute alone with my girlfriend?"*. Hazel was stunned by Trent's word while Callie looks at Hazel and says, *"I'll explain everything later."* Hazel leaves as Trent come closer to Callie and asks, *"have you been with anyone last night?"*. Callie felt nervous as Trent says, *"tell me because my mind is having all sorts of jealousy thoughts and I can't see you with another man."* Callie gets annoyed and says, *"haven't I made it clear to you that I haven't been with anyone man?"*. Trent asks about the party as Callie says, *"I was with Hazel, and she was with this guy and brother who we had drinks with that's all."* Trent pulls her closer as he says, *"I cannot bear to see you with another man; you're mine Angel."* Callie says, *"I am going to tell you this once ok, I love you Trent and always have done. You have to be able to trust me or our relationship will not work."* Trent kisses Callie as his phone rings, he answers and says, *"Alayna?"*. Trent hangs up the phone as he looks a little worried.

Chapter 16

Callie asks, *"Trent what was that about? Who's Alayna?"*. Trent brushes it off and replies, *"don't worry Angel it's nothing important"*. Trent asks, *"do you trust me, Callie?"*. Callie thinks for a moment and replies, *"I am trying to Trent, but you still feel like a puzzle"*. Trent assures her that he is not hiding anything and says, *"Angel all you need to know is that you are my world."* Callie and Trent share a passionate kiss. Meanwhile Storm was in his apartment, waiting for someone to come as the doorbell rings. Storm answers and says, *"where the hell were you?"*. Rick says, *"Storm my man it's good to see you."* As they catch up Rick asks, *"how come you are back? What have you been doing? Listen mate, the stories I have heard about you are terrifying! Is it true you killed the Boss of the Martinez Mafia, the largest cartel in Italy?"* Storm nods and replies, *"it was ordered by the Prime Minister of Italy! She wanted some information regarding a girl, but the fucker wouldn't talk so I had order to kill him."* Rick says, *"let me guess you are here because of a job right!"*. Storm nods as Rick tells Storm about Trent Reeves and his nightclub as Storm was not happy to hear about Trent when the doorbell rang again. Rick asks, *"are you expecting someone Storm?"*.

Storm says, *"there is only one person besides you that knows this address. My brother Oliver!"* Storm says, *"come in! what are you doing here?"*. Oliver says, *"we need to talk."* As Oliver continues, *"I want to know why you went to Callie's workplace."* Rick was confused as he asks, *"Callie? Who's Callie?"*. Oliver says, *"go on Holden explain everything as I just spoke with Hazel, and she told me you were using her to get to Trent Reeves!"* Rick was stunned while Storm got angry says, *"I don't need to justify myself to you!".* Oliver says, *"you do as Hazel is the girl I like very much, and I don't want her to be involved in your business."* As they argue; Storm says, *"I like her ok and she is my next job!".* Oliver is shocked as he asks, *"what do you mean your next job?".* Storm explains about the job to kill Callie as she is the woman of Trent Reeves. Rick says, *"hold on a second. Callie cannot be important to Trent as he is engaged to Alayna Romano?".* Storm asked stunned, *"are you joking right now?"* Rick shakes his head and explains about the engagement as Storm has a plan to keep Callie safe. Oliver says, *"bro you need to think about this calmly."* Storm asks Rick to prepare documents under the name Holden Wilson as Storm says, *"I am going to offer my services to Trent! I will become Callie's bodyguard and protect her."* Rick asks, *"are you sure she has feelings for you?".* Storm answers *"I will make her fall for me, and I will also let her know of Trent's lies."* Oliver says *"I don't want Hazel to be apart of this and you also don't put yourself in danger bro."*

As Rick helps Storm and Oliver clears the air with his brother. Storm has a plan as he discusses it privately. Later that evening Callie comes to Trent's penthouse holding a small box with treats as she calls Trent's name but no response. Liam says, *"Callie???? What are you doing here?"* Callie replies: *"I want to surprise Trent! Where is he????".* As Liam tries to explain about Trent's location just as a young woman enters and says, *"Liam answer the question, where is Trent?".* Liam is shocked and asks, *"Alayna what are you doing here?".* Callie is confused and looks at Liam asking, *"who is this woman?".*

Chapter 17

The woman says, *"I am Alayna Romano, and you are?"*. Liam thinks, *'Alayna is a complete pyscho if she finds out who Callie is; Callie will be in danger.'* Before Callie can introduce herself; Liam says, *"she's, my girl."* Callie was not pleased as she says, *"what are you talking about? I am not..."* Liam says, *"she's not in love with me yet..."* Alayna rolls her eyes and says, *"it's good you got yourself a girl and about time too. Where's Trent?"*. Callie looks angrily at Liam and says, *"what are you talking about?? What?"* Just then Trent comes in and sees Alayna asking, *"what the hell are you doing in my house?"*. Alayna replies, *"Trent don't be like that I came to see you. it is nice to meet Liam and his new girl."* Trent looks angrily at Liam and says, *"his what???"*. Liam says, *"my girlfriend, Callie!"*. Callie sighs and says angrily pointing to Trent, *"this is too much! Do you know what? Do not call me or look for me ever again, ok? I have had enough!"*. Alayna rolls her eyes while Trent cocks his gun and says, *"get the fuck out of my place right now!"* Alayna says, *"chill Babes I will get going but I will see you soon."* As she blows a kiss; Liam explains to Trent that he called Callie his girlfriend to protect her from danger. Trent understood as Liam went to his room and Trent punched the wall in anger. Trent gets a call from Mason as Trent is alarmed by the news and says, *"what do you mean you lost her? if anything happens to her, you're a dead man."* Mason goes in search of Callie; meanwhile in a flower park late at night Storm is smoking as he thinks of Callie.

As Callie comes and cries; Storm overhears someone crying and turns to see it is Callie. Storm says, "*Callie? What are you doing here?*". Callie was still crying as she says "*Holden if you are following me, just leave me alone! I am not interested in arguing with you right now.*" Storm says, "*I had no idea you were here. I swear I am not following you; how do you know this place.*" Callie replies, "*when I first came to Amsterdam years back after leaving the orphanage, I found this place.*" Storm was stunned and says, "*orphanage?*" Callie nods and says, "*I am not going to share with you my life story! It's not like you are worried by me.*" Storm says, "*don't speak like this Callie! You do matter to me.*" As Callie gets defensive to Storm and says, "*you only want to use me.*" Storm comes closer and says, "*I will tell you why I come to this place; I want to share with you something special and secret. Give me a chance to prove I am not using you.*" Callie sees Storm's eyes in which she sees a softer side; Storm explains about how much this place means to him as Callie talks about her childhood and never really knowing her parents. As Storm comes closer and asks, "*can you let me know why you are here and crying? What did Trent do to you?*". The clouds in the sky rumble as it soon pours with heavy rain and Callie shivers due to the cold. Storm makes her wear his leather jacket as Callie looks into Storm's eyes and says, "*Holden you have to accept this truth that I love Trent.*" As Storm pulls her closer to him, they share an eyelock as he says, "*if you don't feel a connection between us right now, I'll leave you alone and walk away.*" As Storm said some more words to Callie about how she deserves to be loved and treated as a Queen. Callie came closer as they kiss under the rain; a few minutes later Callie stops and she runs off leaving Storm thinking, '*I will fight for you my little firefly*'.

Meanwhile Trent is outside Callie's apartment as he has been trying to call her. Hazel comes and asks, "*what do you think you are doing?*". Trent replies, "*I am here to see my girlfriend*". Hazel laughs and scolds Trent who says, "*you can't speak to me like this. I love Callie.*" Hazel says, "*you made my best friend feel like she is not worth anything. She deserves to be loved and she deserves to be recognised as the most amazing person ever."* Trent nods as they continue to argue saying, *"I will never leave her, and I won't let anybody come between us."* As Hazel continues to argue with Trent; Callie sees Trent outside her apartment; she looks at him angrily saying, *"HOW DARE YOU COME TO MY PLACE? DID I NOT MAKE THINGS CLEAR? I DON'T WANT TO SEE YOU AGAIN".* Trent tries to explain thing calmly and soon notices Callie wearing the jacket thinking, *'to whom could this jacket belong?'.* Meanwhile Alayna came to Seth at his hideout and says, *" Boss nice to see you again."* Seth smiles and says, *"it's great you have come back to help me with the plan."*

Chapter 18

As Trent asks Callie about the jacket; Callie says coldly, *"how is this your concern? As far as I am aware, I am not your girlfriend anymore?"* Trent says, *"can we please talk? I want a chance to explain myself!"*. Hazel opens the door, comes into the apartment while Callie says, *"I will give you two minutes to explain yourself."* As Trent tries to explain about Alayna and Liam covering for him. Callie rolls her eyes, *"I am sick of this excuse! Are you not strong enough to protect me? how do you expect to marry me if you do not even have the decency to tell people I am your girlfriend?"*. As Trent pleads and says, *"Angel You are everything I have, and if I don't do this the right way, the fear of something happening to you is much bigger than my selfish desire to scream who you are for me!"*. Callie heads inside while Trent vows to come back and prove himself as her true lover; as Callie comes inside, she tells Hazel about everything. Hazel says, *"I was wondering who this jacket belongs to."* Callie replies, *"it's Holden's"* Hazel was stunned as Callie explains how she saw Holden and how his words touched her. Callie tells Hazel about Oliver and Holden's family history as Hazel was understanding. Hazel asks, *"how are you feeling right now?"*.

Callie replies, *"I am confused! I know my feelings for Trent are true and deep, but I shouldn't have feelings for Holden."* Hazel tells Callie to go shower and they will watch the movie, '*the notebook*'. Callie hugs Hazel and thanks her for being the best friend ever. Meanwhile late at night in an abandoned scrapyard Storm was with Rick; Rick felt a little scared about the location while Storm says, "*I am waiting on Trent's right-hand man. So, I can talk to him about the job.*" As they talk about other things; Storm starts to mention his feelings and Callie. Rick notices Storm without his leather jacket as Storm tells him about Callie and giving it to her. Liam soon comes to the scrapyard; Storm and Liam talk as Liam is impressed by Storm's knowledge of the Black Panther Mafia as Storm explains his skills and asks for a job in security.

As Liam has a quick thought and replies, "*ok! I will speak to my boss! but wait for my call.*" The next day in the afternoon Trent was in his penthouse drinking in his living room; he was in deep thoughts of Callie as he did not sleep the night. Callie comes in as Trent sees her asking, "*are you really here?*". Callie replies, "*I came here because after thinking about last night I may have overreacted*". As they try to sort things out; Callie say, "*I think I should train so I can defend myself and learn how to handles guns*". Trent says, "*why didn't I think of this before? I can arrange for a bodyguard who will train you up.*"; As Trent remembers he says to Callie; "*Angel I think Liam has found the perfect man to train you who used to work in the army. Once you are strong and ready, we can tell the world our relationship. But Angel you will live here with me as I have all the resources, gym, pool and also a shooting range practise below. What are your thoughts on this?*".

Chapter 19

C allie replies, "*only one condition you keep your bossy attitude to yourself and trust me!*". Trent nods and says, "*as long as he doesn't try to flirt with what's mine and keep it professional, I have no problem!*" Callie says, "*if he isn't professional, I will let you know, but you need to learn to control both your anger and jealousy of yours and remember you still have to earn my trust.*" Trent promises as he comes closer to her saying, "*I thought you would never forgive me or give me another chance Angel.*" Callie replies, "*it's not about forgiveness Trent, it's about me trusting you with my heart.*" Trent assures Callie saying, "*Angel let me tell you, your heart has never been safer;* They kiss passionately as Callie says, "*I have to get to work.*" A few hours later Trent's penthouse office he was having a meeting with Liam regarding the new bodyguard as Trent had some doubt however Liam assured him that the man was the best fit.

Liam asks, "*Boss will you tell her about Alayna?*". Trent replies, "*no it was just a rumour in the Mafia world, and I want Callie to be by my side and I want to prove to her that she is my only Queen!*". Liam hears Trent's love for Callie as Liam thinks, '*their love is unconditional, and I hope Boss's happiness is forever.*' Meanwhile in Storm's apartment he hears the doorbell ring, opens to see Oliver, and says, "*you came here so quick.*" Oliver says, "*I was at Hazel's place, and she lives a few minutes to you*". As Storm asks, "*you don't stay at your place?*". Oliver replies, "*I love sleeping at Hazel's place! I never imagined I would someone as amazing and remarkable as her.*" Storm says, "*I am happy for you brother.*" Oliver says, *"you could find happiness too if you didn't set your eyes on the wrong woman?"*. Storm says, *"why do you say it like that?"*. Oliver says, *"I know Callie seems like a great girl but she's with Trent Reeves. All these years we have been apart brother I have lived in worried or fear that something could happen to you because of your job and who you are."* As Storm tries to compare the situations for Oliver with Hazel; both begin to argue as Oliver stops, *"bro just tell me what you need."* Storm explains his plan with Oliver is not happy with it.

Oliver asks, *"did you get the job to work with Trent Reeves?"*. Storm replies, *"not yet but I have a strong feeling that Liam will call me soon."* Storm's phone rings as he sees it is a private number and answers. Liam says, *"I know you are awaiting my response and I have spoken with my boss, and he has agreed to take you on. however, he has a fixed request!"*. Storm asks, *"what is the request?"*. Liam replies *"you will have to come and live with him and his fiancée"*. Storm face changes in anger as he clenches his fist. Liam says, *"Holden are you still there?"*. Storm replies, *"I'm here. why must I stay in place?"*. Liam says, *"as you will oversee Callie's security, you will also be responsible for training her in self-defence. I will forward you the address to meet Boss tonight and make sure you come on time."*

Chapter 20

Storm ends the call as Oliver looks at Storm's facial expression asking, *"what's wrong bro?"*. Storm replies, *"did you know anything about Callie being Trent's fiancée?"*. Oliver was surprised as he replies, *"no I would have known if this was true, perhaps he plans to ask for her hand."* Storm expression was angry. Oliver asks, *"how do you plan to stop him from proposing to Callie? Will you tell Callie about that girl Alayna Romano?"*. Storm sighs and replies, *"there is no use to splitting them up if Callie still loves Trent. I will win her heart so that she will have to decide, and she will choose me!"*. The next day early morning Callie opens her door and sneaks in as she is surprised to see Hazel waiting for her in the living room. Hazel is mad at Callie for sneaking out asking, *"don't tell me you were with Trent yesterday?"*. Callie was surprised as Hazel says, *"you can't hide anything from your bestie."* Callie says, *"I don't want to fight my feelings for Trent anymore. I want to give us a real chance at happiness otherwise if I let this opportunity go how will I be like in a few years thinking I gave up love?"*. Hazel hugs Callie who says, *"Haze I want you to help me pack; Trent has asked me to move in with him."* Hazel is surprised and says, *"I will help you but if he ever breaks your heart, I will cut him up and feed him to my piranhas"*.

Callie laughs, heads inside as Hazel says, *"hold on a second, will you tell Trent about your kiss with Holden?"* Callie shakes her head and replies, *"no I don't want Holden to be in trouble or worse danger."* Hazel heads to the room as Callie thinks for a moment and then joins Hazel as they pack her luggage. As the evening falls, Storm comes to the penthouse and rings the bell as Liam opens the door and comes in. He looks around and asks, *"is Mr. Reeves in?".* Liam replies, *"Holden you have arrived earlier than expected."* Holden says, *"as you told me not to be late, I wanted to make a good impression."* As Trent comes into the living room, he sees Storm and tells Liam leaves the room to give them some privacy. Storm comes closer to Trent saying, *"Liam has already explained my job and duties Mr. Reeves."* Trent says, *"call me Boss because this is what I am to you."* Storm had a deep thought in his mind, *'what? Just like at this guy! Remember I am doing this for Callie and not him!'.* Trent notices Storm being absent-minded and asks, *"is everything ok Holden? You look worried!".* Storm calms down and says, *"no Boss I am just nervous and it's a pleasure to be working for you."* Trent nod, smile and says, *"I like your attitude and especially all the men who work for me respect me! however, I want to let you know this the job you are doing is the most significant one I have ever given anyone to do."*

Chapter 21

S torm replies, "*whatever is valuable to you Boss also is valuable for me!*". Trent nods and says, "*you will be in charge of the safety of the woman of my life, and should anything ever happen to her; you won't live another day.*" Storm nods and replies "*you have nothing to worry about Boss I will guard her with my life.*" Trent also explains Callie's training program as he says, " *the sooner she is trained we can get wed.*" Storm thinks, '*wed? I think not.*' Trent also gives a warning to Storm and says, "*make sure you keep your distance from her because I notice even a small move that you are stepping over your boundaries, I will kill you.*" Storm nods and thinks, '*even if I die trying to win her heart then I don't care.*' Trent asks, "*do you have any questions?*". Storm asks, "*do you and Miss Callie live in a room together?*". Trent rolls his eyes and replies, "*the fewer questions you ask the better.*"

Just as they are talking the doorbell rings as Callie comes in with her suitcase and says, "*Trent I have some more of my stuff downstairs? Can you ask Liam to get it to please?*". Trent says, "*Angel, I will get Liam to handle it; come here I have someone I would like you to meet*". Callie replies, "*is he my new bodyguard?*". Trent nods as Storm turns around and says, "*Miss Callie, it's an honor to meet you! I am Holden and I will be your new bodyguard*". Callie was in shock while Trent came over to Callie asking, "*Angel?? Are you ok?*". As Liam brings up all of Callie's bags; Liam says, "*I can't believe a girl can have so many bags.*" Trent says, "*Liam show Holden his room.*" As Storm leaves to go he winks at Callie who thinks, *'I am so confused as to what I need to do. Should I tell Trent who he is? He makes me shiver just by looking at me, but I need to block out these feelings because I only love Trent and he should only be the one in my heart.'* As Trent sees Callie in deep thoughts; he asks her, *"Angel you look tired, I know this seems like a lot and you're new to all of this, but I want you to feel relaxed and I want to make sure you are taken care of."* Trent continues, *"if you have any problem with this guy or he is not good I will fire him."* Callie nods as she says, *"just give me a few days Trent"*. Callie thinks, *'I have to find out what is on Holden's mind?"*. Callie says, *"I will begin train tomorrow morning."*

As Trent comes closer to Callie to kiss her; she says, *"Trent we said we would take things slowly. I'm feeling very tired and want to go rest."* As Callie heads down the corridor, Trent wonders, *'I hope Callie is not shutting me out again'*. As Callie is about to head into her room, she opens the door to the room next door just as Storm comes out in a towel around him. Callie comes in and turns as Storm smirks asking, *"Callie my little firefly what are you doing here?"*. Callie replies, *"can't you put some clothes on?"*. As Storm tries to talk dirty with her, he comes closer to Callie, pulls her arm turning her to face him as Callie looks at Storm and they share an eye lock.

Chapter 22

Callie had a lot of deep thoughts in her head about Storm. Storm noticed Callie was lost in thoughts as he held her, Storm then broke the silence and asked, *"do you like what is in front of you or should I show you more?"*. Callie replies, *"what I want to know is what sick game do you think you are playing? Why are you here?"*. Storm replies, *"I am not playing any games firefly! I want you."* Callie was stunned and shocked as she says, *"you want me?? I thought I made myself perfectly clear that I love Trent and I am with him."* Storm says, *"forget what you told me! you don't know what you want or else you wouldn't have kissed me."* Callie laughs as she says, *"kissing you was a mistake and don't worry I won't plan on doing it again."* As Storm comes closer to her, he says *"let's cut a deal firefly? I will not kiss you either, but I know at some point you will beg me to point where you will be unable to resist me!* Callie looks at Storm as she asks, *"what if I leave this room right now and say to Trent everything about us?."*

Storm does not feel intimidated or threatened as he replies calmly, *"you are free to go and tell him right now if you like! But we both know between us if you had wanted me out of this penthouse, you could have told him who I was. but you did not do you know why? because your heart feels something for me."* Callie stares at Storm as she replies, *"I didn't tell him anything because I wanted to know what you are up to! and listen to Holden if you are here to harm Trent, I will harm you!"*

Storm looks at her as he says, "*when the time comes Callie, your heart, soul, and mind will choose me. I am doing this job for one reason to make you realize your true feelings. If your heart absolutely loves Trent and as you claim to love him; nothing will be able to tear you apart not even me or fate.*" Callie looked at Storm still processing his words as she sighs and looks at Holden "*you can remain here, as long as you keep things professional and don't try anything.*" Holden lets go of her as he looks her in the eyes and replies, "*I give you my word that I will never lay a finger or touch you without your consent.*" Callie smiles, just before there is a knock on the door as Callie turns and hears Trent's voice calling from outside the door, "*Holden?? Are you awake?*" Callie turned to look back at Storm with a panicked expression on her face. Holden noticed the expression on Callie's face as she thought, '*what should I do?*'.

Chapter 23

As Trent knocks on the door again, Callie is panicking as Storm says, *"give me a minute."* Storm looks around and then whispers to Callie; *"firefly goes hide in the bathroom and calm down."* Callie felt worried and replies, *"what if Trent sees us together like this, he will..."* Storm takes her arm and puts her in the bathroom as he tells her to keep quiet. She nods as he closes the door. Trent opens the door as Storm is still in the towel; Trent asks, *"did you just have a bath?."* Storm nods as Trent says *"I just wanted to check if you are still up for training Callie tomorrow. I will ask one of my men to give you a tour around the penthouse and also access to our gun supplies."*

Trent explains a few more things as Storm nods and says, *"thanks Boss I'll see you tomorrow early."* Trent leaves the room as Storm checks for a few seconds and opens the bathroom door and says, *"coast is clear my firefly."* Callie comes out annoyed as she says, *"you have to leave Holden as you are placing yourself in danger."* Storm is touched by Callie's gesture and says, *"I think it's sweet you care about me."* Callie rolls her eyes as she says, *"I don't care about you, I don't want to be the cause of your death."* As Storm tries to explain how much Callie means to him; Callie says, *"I am going to bed."* Meanwhile later in the evening in the Prime Minister's office Sabrina hears a knock on the door as she says, *"enter!".*

As the person enters the room; Sabrina's expression changes as she says, *"what do you think you are doing here?"* The old woman says, *"please*

I want to talk!" Sabrina is not interested in hearing what the old woman has to say; however, Scarlett pleads and begs for forgiveness. Sabrina asks, *"how do you expect me to forgive you after what you did 20 years back? Do you know how hard it has been for me thinking of my baby girl wondering if she is alive or dead?"* Scarlett says sadly, *"I could never forget her eyes and now it's like I am finally facing a punishment. I have terminal cancer and I am in my last stage; I don't know how much time I have left."* Sabrina is stunned to hear her mother's word as she comes over and wipes Scarlett's tears. Sabrina tells Scarlett of her plan to locate Sophia; as Scarlett prays to meet her granddaughter; Scarlett is about to leave just as Sabrina says, *"mom you can stay with me, and I will try to find some hope of helping you get better and staying alive because you're my family."* They both embrace each other.

Chapter 24

S abrina says, "*mom, anger, hate, and rage has taken me to a dark place, and knowing that you are very ill, I am feeling so guilty for everything.*" Scarlett says, "*I deserve what I am getting but you know I never stopped following you; making sure you were safe and seeing your career to become the first woman Prime Minister of Italy.*" Sabrina smiles as Scarlett feels tired; she calls her secretary Ben who comes in as she says, "*Ben, I would like you to arrange a special room for my mom.*" Scarlett leaves with Ben as she calls Nate in who asks, "*did you require my service, Miss Prime Minister?*". Sabrina nods and says "*prepare the plane! We will be flying to Amsterdam.*"

Nate is unsure of any meetings or conferences as Sabrina says, "*we are going to meet Trent Reeves*"; Nate was doubtful and tried to convince Sabrina not to go. Sabrina had her foot down firmly and says, "*I don't care about anything else, my only aim to becoming the Prime Minister was to locate my daughter, and if going to see Trent Reeves will give me assurance of this I must go.*" Nate nods as he heads out as Sabrina gets dressed and prepares for her flight to Amsterdam. On the plane, Sabrina gives orders to Nate to make sure that everything is prepared as it will be a surprise visit; The next day Trent comes to the kitchen and is surprised to see Callie up early. As Trent flirts with Callie, he comes closer to her and says, "*my beautiful Angel did I ever tell you how sexy you look in your workout clothes?*".

Trent tries to mention her clothes; Callie sighs and says, *"Trent please don't try to control me. I want to wear what I want whenever."* As Trent softens and says, *"you are making me hungry for you."* Trent pulls Callie in for a passionate kiss as Storm comes into the kitchen; he is stunned to see Callie kissing Trent. He has a sad expression on his face; Callie breaks the kiss and reminds Trent that they should be taking their relationship slow; Trent looks at Storm saying, *"Holden what a surprise? Are you going to say something or keep listening to our conversation?"*. Storm apologizes as Trent snaps at Storm however Callie calms Trent down. As Callie tells Trent what she plans to do after her training, Trent smiles and says, *"I'll give you a call later today, Angel, I love you."*

They share another kiss as Trent heads to the nightclub; Storm comes over and he says, *"firefly you didn't have to speak in my favor. I am not afraid of Trent"*. Callie rolls her eyes as Storm says, *"let's begin your training at the gym."* Meanwhile in Romano's base, Alayna was speaking with Seth about Trent. Seth says, *"Trent Reeves has currently got a thing going on with Callie Dawson."* Alayna asks shocked, *"what the hell?"*. Seth says, *"calm yourself, don't worry she will die soon. I have already got her life signed to the hitman Storm."* Alayna smirks evilly as Seth laughs. Back in training Storm was shouting at Callie, trying to intimidate her by calling her pathetic. Callie felt anger as she yelled back; *"WHO THE HELL DO YOU THINK YOU ARE? DON'T YOU DARE CALL ME PATHETIC AND WEAK?"*. Callie took a moment to breathe, grabbed her water bottle as Storm gave her a cold look. Callie wondered; *'what is Holden's problem?'*.

Chapter 25

S torm says in a cold tone, *"I was instructed to teach you to defend yourself as swiftly as possible; the quicker you are stronger and learn, you won't have to wait for your wedding."* Callie looks at Storm and says, *"Oh so I see what you are trying to do? It is not about my training or learning self-defence. You are doing this to spite me and Trent."* Callie gets up, comes closer to Storm and says, *"did I not make myself clear to you I love only Trent?".* As Callie turns; Storm pulls her arm and spins her to him as he holds her close as they stare into each other eyes. Callie thinks, *'this is so wrong but why is my body unable to pull away from him?'.*

Storm looks at her as he still holds her and says, *"I can feel her close to me, she is driving me crazy. I do not want to hear Trent's name on her lips only mine".* As Callie is speechless for a few minutes; Storm says, *"if you want my firefly, I can make you mine here right now."* He whispers into her ears as Callie pushes him and says, *"stop your dirty and seductive words."* However, Storm pulls her back as she looks at him and asks *"why have you come into my life? I told you I only have feelings for Trent, and I don't need you confusing my thoughts and emotions."* Storm assures her, *"I can see your body and lips, they want me, but you are not giving us a chance."* Callie says, *"whatever this is, I don't want my life to be like a movie or love triangle and someone will get injured in the end."* Storm says, *"you must know that we cannot choose who to love! If I could turn off my feelings, I would have done it a long time ago, but I won't because you make me feel alive."* Callie feels conflicted by Storm's word as she says, "*Holden please, I feel like I am in between both of you and this is not right."* Storm caresses her face while she closes her eyes and feels his touch however Callie says, "*I have to go."*

Callie runs out as Storm watches her leave. As his phone rings, he answers, "*what the hell do you want?"*. Seth says, "*watch your tone with me Storm! I want you to meet me in my house in 10 minutes or else."* Storm ends the call as he rolls his eyes and angrily thinks, *'who the fuck does this guy think he is? I will end him once I finish this job'.* Meanwhile, Callie had showered, came to the bakery to see Hazel who was sorting some documents and finishing some calls. As Hazel sees Callie coming in, she says "*I have some good news our loan and bakery has been approved in Berlin."* Callie was excited and says, "*I guess I will have to prepare my bags for the flight."* Hazel says, "*not so fast I am coming with you."* As Hazel notices Callie's is feeling tensed; she comes out and says, "*Maisie me and Callie will be out for a few hours hope you will be ok."* Hazel takes Callie to the Mall to do some shopping and soon get lunch at the Italian restaurant. Hazel asks, "*Callie tell me what's up?"*. Callie replies, "*I feel like my life is like The Vampire diaries right now."* Hazel says, "*you mean you have Stefan and Damon after you."* Callie rolls her eyes sighs, and says, "*last night I met my new bodyguard, and you wouldn't believe who it is?"*. Hazel thinks for a moment while Callie tells her it is Holden. Hazel is stunned as Callie tells her everything; Hazel does not know what to say as Callie says, "*I am so confused because I have Holden on one side making me feel so many things, I never thought I would ever feel and then there's Trent who is my childhood love."* Hazel asks, "*are you sure you don't want to tell Trent anything especially about you and Holden?"*. Callie answers, "*there is no me and Holden. I know how Trent can react in certain situations and I do not want anyone to suffer because of me."* Hazel says, "*well this trip to Berlin will be the best way to relax and think about what you want."* Meanwhile Storm comes to the Romano's hideout as he knocks on the door as Seth says, "*Enter!"*.

Chapter 26

As Storm comes into Seth giving him a cold expression asking, *"what the fuck do you think you have been doing?"*. Storm looks at him as he says, *"don't ever think about intimidating me again! if I want right this second, I can ruin your reputation in the Mafia world. Remember your place!"*. Storm has an angry expression as Seth thinks, *'he is the only one that can do this job.'* Seth says, *"I am losing my mind as the bitch is still living"*. Storm clenches his fist in anger however he says to Seth; *"if you feel like I am taking along with the job, go and find another hitman."* Storm tells Seth of his plan and asks for time, Seth listens to the plan. Meanwhile, at Trent's apartment, Liam comes; he gets a phone call from Trent as Trent says, *"Liam, is Callie and Holden there?"*. Liam checks the room and calls out their names as it is quiet however just then the doorbell rings. Liam opens the door and is stunned to see it is the Prime Minister. Liam informs Trent as he hangs up; Liam says, *"Miss Prime Minister it's a privilege to meet you."* Sabrina thanks him as she comes in with her security as Sabrina says, *"I am here to meet Trent Reeves."*

Just then Callie comes in and looks around wondering what is going on. Callie sees Liam and says, *"what's going on here? are you ok?"*. Sabrina was stunned by the voice as Liam looked at Sabrina and Callie and wondered, *'they look so alike; I must be imagining things as I haven't slept much lately.'* As Callie talks with Liam, Sabrina turns to see Callie as she has a lot of thoughts running through her head; *'people may call me crazy but seeing this girl in front of me; her eyes and voice are familiar. I need more proof before making a statement.'* Callie says, "*I recognize you; you're the prime minister of Italy.*" Sabrina says, "*it's lovely to meet you. who might you be?*". Liam steps in and says, "*Miss Sabrina this is Callie, and she is Trent's fiancée!*". Callie did not know but she was a little stunned to see Sabrina saying, "*I am feeling a little nervous, I've never met anybody in such a high-profile person as yourself.*" Liam says, "*Trent should be back shortly, would you like a cup of tea or anything?*". Sabrina nods and says, "*that would be lovely thanks Liam*"; Callie had some thoughts running through her mind as she says, "*I'd better start packing; notify me once Trent has come back, please Liam.*"

Liam nods as Sabrina takes a seat and he heads to the kitchen to make tea. Callie waves to Sabrina who smiles at her. As Sabrina calls over Nate she asks, "*did you notice something just now between me and Callie? I would like you to find out about this girl.*" Sabrina thinks, '*I have more than a feeling that this girl could be my daughter.*' Back in Rick's apartment, he was having fun with a woman named Tia as Storm kicked the door down. Rick and Tia jumped behind the sofa as Storm came in as Rick says, "*what the hell bro?*". Storm rolls his eyes and tells Rick to get rid of his girl. As Tia kisses Rick, Rick says, "*I'll call you baby doll.*" Storm closes the door and says, "*we need to talk.*" Storm tells everything about the plan and what happened at the Romano's base earlier. Rick says, "*you are playing a dangerous game Storm.*" Storm rolls his eyes and tells Rick more about the plan. Rick asks, "*you are not still thinking of killing Trent.*" Storm replies, "*of course not, and neither will I attack nor kill Callie. I already told you I plan to win her heart and get her to fall in love with me.*"

Chapter 27

Liam brings a tea and biscuit just as Trent comes in. He sees Sabrina and says, *"Sabrina, what a pleasure to have you in my place. How can I help you?"*. Sabrina stands up and apologies as she says, *"I have something to discuss with you."* Trent understands as he says, *"coming all the way must be very significant"*. As they talk, Sabrina says *"Trent earlier I met your fiancée Callie earlier and I don't know why but I feel she is associated."* Trent had a lot of doubt in his mind however he soon said, *"Callie's parents are dead, any suspicion you may have please forget about them."* Sabrina had a painful expression on her face as she says, *"I am sorry to hear that, have you found any updates on my daughter's case?"*. Trent replies, *"I am in the process of getting information and will let you know in due course."* Sabrina gives a one-week deadline to Trent as she leaves and says, *"I understand and know you are a man of your words. I look forward to hearing from you soon Mr. Reeves."*; Trent thinks, *'I want to clear any doubt she may have that Callie is not her daughter.'* As she leaves Trent calls Liam and he asks Liam, *"do you think there may be any resemblance to Callie and Sabrina?"*. Liam says, *"I did have a feeling when I saw them together."* As Liam asks, *"Boss are you sure there's no chance they might be related?"*. Trent replies *"no because even if there is, Callie is not going to go through the pain I have gone through."*.

Trent gives Liam instructions to prepare for Italy. Trent comes to Callie's bedroom as he finds her packing her bag asking, *"Angel where are you going?"*. Callie asks, *"has the prime minister left? I have just finished packing"*. Trent nods as Trent says, *"hang on a sec, what do you mean packing? Where are you going, Angel?"*. Callie replies, *"Hazel and I are heading to Berlin as we have opened a new bakery there."* As Trent says, *"you cannot go, Angel, I have to fly to Italy this evening for some business."*. As they have an argument Trent sighs as Callie says, *"Trent, I told you I can't give my life and live in fear forever."* Trent nods and says, *"Holden will be accompanying you on the trip."* Trent tells Callie she can take one of his private planes as Callie says, *"me, Hazel and Holden will be flying out tomorrow morning. The trip should only be a week."* Callie asks about Trent's meeting with the Prime Minister of Italy. Trent does not go into details but just says, *"Angel I have a deal with her, don't worry."* Callie sighs and says *"Trent, you might call me crazy but seeing the woman I don't know why I felt like she's related to me. seeing her made me think of my parents."* Trent says, *"don't worry about all that now."* Callie asks, *"when you come back, do you think you can help me find my parent's grave?"*. Trent nods as he kisses her and leaves. Callie phones Hazel who asks, *"hey bestie did you get the tickets ready?"* Callie replies, *"don't worry about that. it's sorted."* As Trent came out, he saw Storm as Storm asked, *"Boss is everything ok?"*.

Chapter 28

Trent looked annoyed as he warns Storm and says, "*Holden you better keep your distance with Callie and be professional, If I even see one thing happening, I will kill you.*" Storm assures Trent who says, "*now that it is all cleared up, I wanted to inform you that you will be flying out with Callie to Berlin tomorrow.*" Trent gives Storm some orders as Storm nods and says, "*you don't need to worry Boss, I will guard her with my life.*" As Storm heads to his room and begins to pack Liam comes and says, "*Boss the plane is almost ready to leave.*" Meanwhile, on the plane trip back to Italy, Sabrina did not know but she had a feeling that Callie could be her daughter; she soon falls asleep as they head back to the office. Later, Sabrina is working on some documents a knock on the door interrupts her thoughts as she says, "*enter!*". Nate comes in holding a brown file and says, "*Madam as you requested here is the file on Callie Dawson*". Sabrina thanks him and sees the file but is stunned to see it does not contain Callie's childhood information. Nate says, "*it shows everything from her 20 years and later.*" Sabrina says, "*there is something skeptical about this. I need to look into this person.*" Nate asks, "*Prime minister shouldn't we wait for information from Reeves?*".

Sabrina gives him instructions as Nate nods and leaves. Meanwhile, on the plane, Liam was preparing for what is to come next. As Trent is working on his laptop; Liam says, "*Boss we don't have an accurate location of where the two people who kidnapped the girl are. We have only a place; Tuscany.*" Trent was annoyed and says, "*I have only a week,*

I gave my word and promise Sabrina that I would sort and find out where her daughter is." Trent seemed more annoyed as Liam had more information on the location being used by secret Mafia cartels. Trent says, *"I am risking my life for this!"* Liam says, *"Boss if you want to head back now, we can and arrange some men to go and locate them."* Trent shakes his head and says, *"I must do this and after today this mission has become personal."* Liam is confused as he asks, *"Boss what is it? are you having second thoughts that Callie could perhaps be the prime minister's daughter?"*. Trent explains his fears and doubt as he says, *"Callie has also asked for my help to locate her parents graves. I just hope I am able to clear the path."* Liam looks at Trent and says, *"Boss if she does belong to the prime minister what will you do?"*. Trent says," *I won't let her go because all these years have affected her; I am her family now and I am protecting her from feeling unwanted and abandoned."*

Liam feels sad and prays that everything will be ok; meanwhile back in Berlin; Hazel, Storm, and Callie checked into the hotel. Hazel says, *"we have a day to explore Berlin before checking out the bakery tomorrow."* As they freshen up; Callie, Hazel, and Storm explore Berlin and enjoy the food; as Callie heads to the restroom. Hazel enjoys the dessert and talks with Storm; she warns him not to hurt Callie. Storm says, *"I am not playing any games, I want her to experience what love really is."*. Hazel mentions a small bit of Callie's childhood and mentions that Callie has never been with any man. Hazel says, *"Callie only wishes for honesty in a relationship and if you or Trent ever hurt or betray her. she will be broken, and I will kill either of you. she's a pure soul."* As Hazel gets a call from Oliver she gets up and takes it as Callie comes back. Storm says, *"Hazel is on the phone with Oliver."* As they talk Holden comes closer to Callie and whispers; *"firefly I know you haven't been with any man, and you must know that I will forever wait for you."* Callie was stunned while Storm has a playful smirk on his face.

Chapter 29

Later that evening Callie confronts Hazel in her room. Hazel asks, *"what are you mad at me for? For telling Holden that you are still a virgin?"*. Hazel says, *"I care about you Callie and I want you to have the best future. But you are avoiding feelings and then accusing me of sorts is not going to help you"*. Callie says, *"he's doing my head and mixing my emotions."* Hazel says, *"why don't I call Trent and tell him about Holden and your relationship?"*. Callie replies, *"Holden and me are not in a relationship and Trent shouldn't know anything please."* Hazel sighs and says, *"ok Calls as you wish but please let's not discuss this."* Callie asks, *"so how's your relationship with Oliver going?"*. Hazel replies *" very well."* Hazel discusses a private matter with Callie; she agrees to the plan for three days time. Meanwhile in Tuscany in the woods; Trent, Liam, and a few more men were waiting as Trent asks, *"Is everyone in position and ready?"*. Everyone says, *"yes Boss!"*. Trent thinks: *'I hope they are here, and this will clear all my fears and suspicions'*.

Trent gives the men positions to stand at as Liam asks, *"Boss have you called Callie?"*. Trent replies, *"not yet I can't speak to her now, I am not leaving Italy without the truth."* The next day Hazel and Callie come to the new bakery as everything is arranged; Hazel investigates the office while Callie sees the kitchen. Hazel makes some phone calls as Callie prepares a batch of cupcakes and cookies. Just as she finishes and puts them out a young woman comes in. She sighs as Callie asks, *"hold on"*. Callie brings some water as the woman drinks it and thanks to her; Callie asks, *"how may I help you?"*. As she introduces herself, *"I'm Aria and I am here for the job as the manager of the business?"*. Callie was surprised as Hazel came out. Hazel sees Aria as Callie says, *"Aria is here for an interview."* As they come into the office; Aria gives her CV to Hazel while Callie sees Aria is nervous and says, *"you don't need to be nervous."* Hazel and Callie ask a few questions about her experience and knowledge as Callie says, *"you're hired."* Aria thanks and says, *"I will start from tomorrow."* As Hazel and Callie talk, Aria runs out of the bakery down the road however bumps into Storm; she apologizes while Storm asks, *"are you ok?"*.

Aria nods as she says, *"I'd better get home it's getting late."* Storm offers her a lift however Aria says, *"I am sure you are waiting for someone."* As Hazel and Callie come out from the bakery down the road; Callie is not happy seeing Aria and Storm together and wonders, *'why I am feeling envious just seeing Aria close to Holden?'*. Callie says, *"if you are quite finished flirting Holden can we go now?"*. Aria apologizes as she runs off to catch the bus; as they head back to the hotel; Hazel sees Callie pacing the room. Callie says, *"I told you he was just fooling around with me. he was flirting with that girl."* Hazel sighs and asks, *"are you sure you are not jealous?"*. Callie sighs and says, *"no I am not, I just hate being played around; first Trent who is not returning my calls and then there's Holden?"*. Storm comes in as Hazel goes out to give them some privacy. Callie says, *"I don't want to see you here."* Storm comes closer to her and says, *"firefly there's no other woman that could take your place in my heart, please believe me."* As they have an eye lock; Callie says, *"I am feeling tired now and have a busy day tomorrow."*

Chapter 30

Back in Tuscany outside a small farmhouse, Trent's men had surrounded the area as Liam speaks with Trent and says, *"I can see two people inside."* Trent says *"Liam, only you and I are to enter."* Trent looks at Liam and asks, *"are you prepared for this?"*. Liam replies, *"yes Boss I am ready!"*. Inside the farmhouse lived two elderly couple a woman named Ellis and a man named John as they were both talking about the necessities of the house running low. Liam kicked the door down as John held a gun while Trent came in pointing his gun along with Liam. Trent says, *"if you put your gun down, I might give your life a few more minutes to live."* John angrily turns to Trent and asks, *"who do you think you are? Was it the Prime minister that sent you?"*. Trent says, *"you are not the one to ask questions understand!"*. Ellis is feeling frightened as Liam ties them up. He looks at John and says, *"you want to know who I am? I am Trent Reeves, Leader of the Black Panther Mafia"*. John acts and says, *"we are nobody special, why have you come after us?"*. Trent fires at the wall as he says, *"don't try to act smart with me! just answer me this; I want you to tell me what you know about the current Prime minister daughter of Italy."*

As John explains about the order to kill the little girl; Trent feels anger boiling up as John says, *"we had to make a decision for our lives it was either us or her?"*. Ellis pleads Trent to spare them as Trent cocks his gun and kills John; Ellis cries for her husband as Trent says, *"don't be so sad I will make you join him."* Ellis says, *"hold on the girl is not dead!"*.

Trent was stunned as he dropped his gun; back at the Romano base; Seth was on the phone to someone as he gave orders not to return as Alayna came in and says, "*Boss I just spoke with my brother Kevin, when will he be able to come back?*". Seth says, "*I miss your brother too, but it is still not safe.*" As Vyom comes in and says, "*Boss we need to talk.*" Alayna goes outside as Seth says, "*have you got any updates on Storm regarding the mission?*". Vyom had doubts as he explained whether Storm was still on their side or if he had betrayed them. Vyom says, "*Boss I think we should take matters into our own hands; as the sooner Trent Reeves is dead the sooner your son can come back home.*" As Seth gives Vyom some instructions and also says "*you must ensure that Storm has no knowledge of this*". Alayna overhears the plan from outside as she thinks about Trent, *'very soon we will meet again'.*

Chapter 31

As Trent demanded the woman speak; Ellis took a deep breath and told Trent that the girl was alive as she says, *"John my husband never knew about this but the day he told me to kill the girl, I couldn't bring myself to do the request and so I told my cousin Lina to take her to the orphanage; at first Lina had doubts however she changed the girl's name"*. Trent was shocked as Ellis says, *"wherever this girl is now her name would be Callie Dawson."* Trent is shocked and screams, *"NOOOOOOO this cannot be."* Ellis begs and swears that what she is saying is the truth as she says, *"you may kill me not but that doesn't change that Callie Dawson real name is Sophia Anderson"*. As Trent cocks the gun on her; Liam comes back in as he asks, *"Boss what is happening?"*. As Trent says, *"she has just told me that Callie's real name is Sophia Anderson. Do you know what this implies?"*. Liam says, *"Boss, Callie is the daughter of the prime minister"*. As Trent turns to Liam and tries to shush him; Liam says, *"Boss, think about this calmly, they look alike and share the same features."* Trent gives orders to take Ellis as they leave; a few hours pass in the hotel room as Trent is still in shock after finding out the truth. Liam comes in as Trent says, *"I said I do not wish to be disturbed."*

Liam notices that Trent is deep shocked and tries to assure him that everything will be ok; Trent asks, *"how can everything be, ok? What should I tell my Angel?"*. Trent says, *"how will she react hearing that her mom was alive, she was kidnapped and told her parents were dead? I can't lose her."* Liam says, *"Boss I know it's hard, but she will be able to handle the news and she deserves to be united with her family".* As Trent and Liam are talking; Trent sees Callie's incoming call as Liam tells Trent to answer it. Trent answers and says, *"hey Angel how are you?".* Callie says, *"Trent, you have been avoiding my calls... is everything ok?".* Trent replies, *"Angel I am fine; it's just this business trip has made me so busy with everything."* Callie asks if there is anything wrong however Trent reassures her; Callie says, *"I may stay for a few more days in Berlin as we have opened the new business."* Callie says, *"I miss you and I hope you can come here."* Trent is hesitant as he disconnects the call. Liam asks, *"Boss are you ok? Will you talk with Callie about this?".* Trent sighs saying, *"I don't know."*

Meanwhile, Callie is thinking about Trent being distant and cold on the phone as Hazel comes in and says, *"Callie we have work to do."* As Hazel notices Callie's sadness, they have a chat as Hazel says, *"maybe I should focus on the preparations and you on Holden."* Callie changes as she heads to the bakery and meets with Aria. Aria watches Callie baking and makes notes as she says, *"you are a pro at this Miss Callie."* Aria tries the chocolate chip cookie and lemon cupcake as she says, *"Yummy, delicious."* Callie smiles as she gives Aria some more tips and advice. Later that night Callie wonders how to surprise Storm as the next morning Callie comes out of her room and sees Storm in the kitchen on his phone. Storm says, *"firefly how are you feeling?".* Callie asks, *"what are your plans tomorrow? Would you like to spend the day together?".* Storm was surprised as he looked at her and asks, *"firefly are you inviting me on a date?".* Callie looks awkwardly at Storm.

Chapter 32

As Callie looks at Storm nervously; she says, *"let's not label it."* As Storm says, *"can we not do it for another day?"*. Callie shakes her head and says, *"no, please tomorrow is perfect."* As Callie pleads for Storm not to leave, he comes closer to her; Storm says, *"my little firefly your wish is my command."* Callie is nervous around Storm as, *"Holden look I don't love you or hate you. I share a deep bond with Trent that cannot be erased or forgotten."* As Storm tries to convince her and asks, *"you keep telling me about your feelings for Trent but where do I stand in all of this firefly?"*. Callie is confused as she replies, *"I don't know Holden."* As she tells Storm that she will be out doing shopping and in the bakery for the rest of the day. Holden says, *"I'll see you later."* Callie heads out as she calls Hazel who says, *"Calls come on I am waiting for you at the shop."* Storm phones Rick and cancels his flight to Amsterdam as Storm is also suspicious he has not heard from Trent who is still in Italy. Storm says, *"Rick, I want you to investigate the matter."* Meanwhile in a basement, Ellis is crying and pleading for life as Trent comes and says, *"don't worry I will not kill you because you're the reason for the life."* Ellis is surprised as she asks, *"do you know Sophia?"*. Trent replies, *"I know Callie, she's, my fiancée."*

As they talk more Trent leaves the room as Ellis continues to cry and sob. As the evening falls in Berlin, Aria and Callie have had a wonderful day of sales in the bakery as Aria says, *"Miss Callie today was great. I hope that when you leave soon that I will continue to make the business grow."* Hazel says, *"that's all we want and expect."* As Callie comes outside, she sees Storm smoking and waiting for her. Callie looks at Hazel asking, *"are you sure you want to do the surprise tomorrow?".* Hazel nods. The next day Hazel left early to get the preparations ready as Callie took Storm around the city as they ate lunch and went sightseeing. As the evening came and Callie changed; Storm was on the phone with Rick as Callie came out wearing a red lace dress. Storm says, *"firefly you look stunning?".* Callie smiles as she apologizes for making him wait; Storm says, *"you are worth waiting."* Callie says, *"are you ready?".* As Storm was not sure what was happening, he tried to avoid the subject staying inside; however, Callie walked outside followed by Storm. At the beach outside decorations were put up as Hazel laid the table with the help of Oliver. Oliver says, *"I am so lucky to have you in my life Haze."* As Hazel and Oliver talk, Callie brings Storm as she says, *"Surprise Holden."* As the music starts and people raise their glasses. Storm's expression becomes angry as he says, *"What the hell do you think you all are playing at!".* Oliver notices Storm's facial expression as pain and says, *"bro I..."*

As Storm turns and leaves; Oliver is about to go after him as Hazel holds his hand and Callie says, *"Oliver I will speak with Holden."* As Callie finds Holden near the lighthouse looking at the sky. Callie comes over as she apologizes and says, *"Holden we all care about you."* Holden was cold and unresponsive as Callie wrapped her arms around Storm. Meanwhile, Oliver was worried for his brother as Hazel said, *"it's my fault".* Oliver looks at her as he wipes her tears and says, *"babes you are not to blame. I love you".* Oliver and Hazel share a kiss; meanwhile, Callie gives some wise words to Storm about life and family. As Storm turns to Callie and asks, *"why are you coming closer to me firefly when you don't know how you feel about me?".* Callie felt Storm's pain as she pulled him closer, and their lips kissed.

Chapter 33

The next day Hazel awoke to see the bed empty beside her as she came to the living room and saw Oliver having coffee. Hazel asks, *"babes you're up early? Are you ok?"*. Oliver tells Hazel he has been worried for Holden since yesterday and says, *"am I a bad brother? I must have hurt him a lot yesterday that is why he is gone?"*. Hazel comes over saying, *"you're a brilliant brother. and I am sure he is ok."* As they talk, Hazel remembers Callie and says, *"I am going to check if Callie's in her room, maybe she can locate Holden"*. Hazel opens Callie's room; she is shocked and stunned to see that Callie is asleep with Storm beside her. Callie wakes up hearing noise and sees Hazel saying, *"we never slept together, last night he was emotional, and we kissed"*. Callie explains a little more to Hazel while Oliver is in the living room wondering if everything is ok. As the doorbell rings, Oliver opens the door to see Trent. Trent looks concerned asking, *"who are you?"*. Oliver introduces himself as Hazel's boyfriend while Trent nods asking, *"do you know where Callie's room is?"*.

Oliver points him in the direction as Oliver calls Hazel and says, *"Emergency Trent is here!"*. As Hazel thanks Oliver for the warning, Hazel says, *"you need to get Holden to leave, Trent is on his way here."* Callie was stunned as Hazel says, *"I will try to get you some time."* Callie panics as Hazel tells her to calm down and heads out; Trent says, *"Angel are you sleeping?"*. Hazel comes and says, *"Trent, Callie is sleeping; business was very tiring yesterday"*. Trent says, *"I wanted to surprise my*

Angel. I have not spoken to her with her for a few days". Hazel gives Trent an idea to plan a special surprise dinner to catch-up. Trent heads to living room as he takes a call; back in Callie's room she wakes Storm up. He looks around and questions Callie, *"what's happening?".* Callie mentions Trent's arrival as Storm gets off the bed angrily saying, *"you've got to be kidding me, these past few days I thought we were coming closer and now you are trying to get rid of me like trash because of him."* Callie says, *"I never intended to treat you like this and I did tell you on several occasions I love Trent and he is the only one who has my heart."* Storm says, *"so I am ok for you to share kisses but to have your heart I can't have it."* Callie felt conflicted and says, *"I think it's better if you leave my life Holden".*

Storm felt sadness hearing Callie's word as he left the room leaving Callie in thoughts. As Trent finished his call with Liam regarding the case; Storm walked in the living room; Trent asks, *"Holden is everything ok?".* Storm nods as he informs that he would like to fly back to Amsterdam. Trent is confused as he ask, *"you know your job is here to protect Callie?".* Storm tries to make an excuse however Trent becomes cold and says, *"you cannot abandon your responsibilities."* Trent gives a demand to Storm as both look at each other angrily.

Chapter 34

T rent and Storm are both arguing; Callie sees Trent asking surprise, *"Trent? What is happening?"*. Trent turned to see Callie as he came over and says, *"Angel, are you feeling, ok?"*. Callie wanted to know what Trent was up to. Trent assured her, *"Holden and I are just clearing up things"*. As Trent informs Callie that Storm wants to go; Callie says, *"Trent let Holden go."* Trent is stunned however tells Storm to leave. Storm leaves while Trent explains the procedure however Callie says, *"Trent I have been worried about you."* Trent comes closer to Callie asking, *"how about we do something special tonight just me and you? how does dinner sound, Angel?"*.

Callie nods as they share a kiss; Callie has a lot of deep thoughts however pulls Trent closer to her. Trent breaks the kiss, he says *"I am going to head for a shower and get some rest"*. Callie nods and says, *"I am going to the bakery"*. As Trent headed towards the shower; Callie freshened up and went to the bakery as she tried to focus on the business; however, her mind was still thinking that Trent was hiding something. Meanwhile Hazel is on the beach with Oliver as they are talking about Callie and Storm. Oliver says, *"babes thanks for helping Holden out. if Trent had found him with Callie, then..."* Hazel comes closer to Oliver explaining that she is always there for him. Hazel says, *"Callie is also my best friend, and of course I would never want her to get hurt."* Oliver had doubts about Storm's relationship; however just then Storm came to the beach and informed Oliver and Hazel that he was heading back to Amsterdam. Oliver asks, *"bro what do you mean you are leaving?"*. Storm replies, *"I know that there's no point in fighting for a girl who doesn't feel the same for me."* Just then Storm gets a call from Rick as they talk however Storm's expression becomes cold as he says, *"Rick what are you saying?"*. Rick replies, *"Seth is planning to attack Trent Reeves! I don't know but he has rumored that you are not doing your job."* Storm says, *"I will manage things here."* Storm says, *"I have still my work cut out here."*

Storm explains to Oliver and Hazel what is happening. Hazel gets worried for Callie as Storm says, *"don't worry nothing will happen to her or Trent."* Later that evening Callie was in deep thoughts of over Storm as a knock on the door interrupted her. Callie says, *"come in."* Trent came in a black suit while Callie finished her makeup as they talked; Trent asks, *"Angel are you ready to head out?"*. Callie nodded and they left. In the restaurant Callie enjoyed the delicious food while Trent watched her and smiled. Callie noticed Trent looking at her who says, *"you are the sexiest Angel in the world."* Callie blushes as he continues saying, *"I want to do this with you, take you on dinner dates, movies and hold you in my arms forever."* Callie tells Trent, *"I also want the same with you Trent, marriage, kids and a future."* Callie looks sadly at Trent saying, *"I want us to have the best relationship and that means no secrets or lies."* Trent says, *"Callie, you're scaring me, is everything ok?"*. Callie says, *"I've kissed someone twice."* Trent's face changed to anger as he wanted to know who it was however Callie refused to give the name. Callie tried to assure him that she only wants him however Trent felt conflicted, pain and says, *"I feel suffocated, I am heading out for some fresh air."* Callie had tears in her eyes and wondered, *'is fate going to break me and Trent again?'*

Chapter 35

As Trent was outside angry; he fired his gun to the wall as he used all his bullets to release his anger and frustration; Callie came outside and saw Trent, she felt so many emotions as she said, *"Trent, please look at me"*. Trent turns with sadness in his eyes to Callie who comes closer to him, he pushes her against the wall as they share an eye lock. Trent says, *"you're my Angel and I can't stand any man having you"*. Callie brings Trent closer and says, *"I am not just your Angel but your family."* As they kiss; an unknown figure points a gun, and a shot is fired. Callie is stunned and shocked to see Storm on the floor covered in blood; As Callie cries uncontrollably; Trent checks to see if she is ok however Callie pleads with Trent to help save Storm. Callie bends down and says, *"Holden you are going to be ok. Stay with me."*

Trent bend down and check Storm's pulse he says, *"it's getting weaker."* Callie calls for an ambulance while Trent sees Callie's care for Storm. Trent thinks and wonders, *'it can't be, right?'.* As they get to the hospital Callie calls Hazel who is with Oliver. Hazel says, *"What? what do you mean hospital?".* Oliver asks, *"babes what's wrong? what happened?".* Hazel and Oliver rush to the general hospital and wait outside. Oliver asks, *"what did you do to my brother? This is all your fault."* Callie says, *"Oliver, Holden is in surgery and his condition was critical."* Oliver shouts and blames Callie for everything and says, *"you are not worthy of my brother's love or affections".* Callie cries while Hazel says, *"enough Oliver stop hurting my best friend; if you can't respect Callie then we have no future".* Oliver heads out while Callie looks at Hazel saying, *"Haze you should go after him."* Hazel says, *"you come first. Tell me what happened".* Callie tells Hazel everything about the dinner, shooting. Hazel says, *"I can't believe you told Trent about the kiss".* Callie replies, *"I wanted an honest relationship and no lies or secrets".*

Hazel hugs Callie while Trent is outside smoking and thinking about everything; as Liam comes to Trent he asks, *"Boss are you ok?".* Trent nods and asks Liam to get a background check on Holden Wilson. Liam asks, *"Boss why are you asking me this?".* Trent replies, *"he saved my life, but he also kissed my girl."* As Trent heads inside; A few hours later Oliver comes back, sees Hazel and they have a talk. Oliver says, *"I can't do this Haze; my brother means the world to me. he's my only family."* Hazel says, *"I understand because Callie is my world and if you ever gave me an ultimatum; I would choose Callie every time".* Oliver says, *"when my brother Holden wakes up, we will go somewhere far away".* Hazel has tears in her eyes as Oliver embraces her. Trent who has overheard their conversation wonders, *'is there more to Holden than meets the eye?'.* Meanwhile, Callie comes into Storm's room, she sees him still unconscious as the doctor comes in; Callie turns to speak to him asking, *"doctor how is he?".* The doctor replies, *"are you family for the patient?".* Callie looks nervously and is about to reply.

Chapter 36

As Callie responds to the doctor saying, *"you could say that."* The doctor gives an update and gives Callie some good news, *"he is young, strong, and will make a full recovery."* Callie looks at Storm and at the doctor asking, *"when will he wake up?"*. The doctor says, *"it could be a few days or tomorrow"*. As the doctor gets paged for another patient, he goes as Callie turns to look at Storm and comes closer, she cries and apologizes for everything. Callie says, *"I never expected you to be caught in the crossfire"*; Trent comes in as he asks, *"Angel this is the dickhead who kissed you?"*. Callie turns to Trent and angrily says *"how dare you! he just saved your life?"*. Trent says, *"I saw how you were when he was shot, the pain and worry on your facial expression told me everything"*. Callie and Trent argue, and she says, *"ok fine I admit it, I have feelings for Holden."* Trent felt pain in his heart hearing her words as Callie says, *"but Trent that doesn't matter because I chose you not him. we are soulmates and regardless of secrets you may hide from me, I love you."*

Trent felt a guilty look over his face as Callie sighed and says, *"I can't do this, I'm exhausted."* Callie leaves the room while Trent was left in deep thoughts As Callie sat in the hotel room after her shower she could not help thinking of Storm. Callie says, *"I hope Holden wakes up soon."* The next morning, Callie comes to the hospital to see Storm and sees the doctor examining him. Callie asks, *"doctor is he better?"*. The doctor nods and says, *"I am sure he will awake soon"*. Callie comes over to Storm, speaks to him and confesses telling Trent about their kiss and relationship. As Callie cries and feels responsible for his condition, a teardrop lands on Storm's face as he stirs and opens his eyes. Callie has a smile saying, *"I will get the doctor."* Storm holds her hand and says, *"firefly please stay with me."* Callie nods as Storm says, *"I heard you confession last night, you like me."* Callie nods and says, *"I do like you Holden, but my heart belongs to Trent."*

Storm sat up as Callie gave him some water. Storm says, *"I would never let anything happen to you or Trent, firefly."* Callie has a small smile on her face asking, *"how are you feeling now?"*. Storm says, *"firefly there's something I need to tell you."* Callie felt nervous as she looked at Storm, *"if you are honest about your feelings, then it's only fair I give you, my truth"*. Callie looked confused by Storm's word; he took a deep breath and says, *"I am not who you think I am firefly. The reason for me being close to you was to protect you"*. Callie says, *"stop talking in riddles Holden and tell me the truth!"*. Storm says, *"my name isn't Holden, it's Storm and I'm a professional hitman"*. Callie was stunned while she listened to Storm explained his services, tasks and also why he came to work for Trent. Callie was shocked and felt anger as she said, *"you're the reason why I could have lost Trent?"*. Storm tries to beg for a chance saying, *"firefly I know this is hard to take in but the reason we met was that I was appointed to end you"*. Callie was in shock and stunned by Storm's words.

Chapter 37

C allie had anger in her eyes as Storm apologizes however Callie punches him and says, *"I can't believe I thought of having feelings for you, you lied to me"*. Storm says, *"firefly please you have understood everything I did was to protect you."* Callie asks, *"just answer me this one question who is responsible for the attack on Trent?"*. Storm replies, *"Seth Romano of the German Cartel Mafia."* Callie says, *"I can't forgive you for lying to me"*. Storm briefly mentions Trent however Callie angrily points at him, *"don't compare yourself to Trent!"*. A couple of hours later Trent comes to the hospital room as he talks with Storm who says, *"Boss I think you should know my truth and that is that I am a professional hitman by the name of Storm"*. As Trent cocks his gun to point at Storm; Storm says, *"I never expected to fall in love with Callie, but I want to make a final promise to end Seth Romano."* Trent was stunned and asks, *"Seth Romano? The Mafia leader of the German Cartel Mafia?"*. Storm nods as he says, *"I know Callie has chosen you, but any lies or secrets you are hiding from her. you should tell her because they will only break you apart."*

As Trent and Storm argue, Storm leaves and says, *"if you ever need me, Boss, I will always be there to help you"*. Trent is left in thoughts; outside Storm calls Oliver and updates him; As Oliver finishes packing his bags he says, *"bro it's probably for the best."* Hazel comes to the living room as Oliver is holding his luggage; Hazel asks, *"babes do you have to leave?"*. Oliver looks at Hazel as their eyes meet however Callie comes in and angrily looks at Oliver. Callie says, *"you and your brother are liars".* Oliver tries to calm Callie down; Callie tells Hazel everything as she looks at Oliver asking, *"what? answer me is what Callie is saying the truth?".* Oliver nods and Hazel pushes Oliver and his suitcase out of the hotel and painfully says, *"I never want to see you again."*

Callie and Hazel talk with each other and hug; later that evening, Callie comes to the lighthouse and looks at the sky; Trent asks, *"Angel how are you feeling?".* Callie has sadness in her eyes as she tells Trent about Storm's truth. Trent tells Callie, *"He told me everything".* Callie comes closer to Trent saying, *"I am sorry for hurting you."* Trent holds her in his arms as Callie says, *"I don't want anything to do with the lying scumbag, but Trent if you are hiding secrets or lies from me...".* Trent kisses Callie just as her phone rings and she answers it. Trent thinks, *'I cannot lose her; I must not tell her about Sabrina or Alayna'.* Later that night; Trent, Hazel, and Callie fly back to Amsterdam while Callie sleeps Trent takes care of her. Hazel says, *"Trent I also want to clear the air between us. I know how much you love my best friend and I want only her happiness".* Trent nod and promises to always be there for Callie.

The next morning back in Amsterdam; Liam is with Sabrina waiting for Trent. Liam says, *"Miss Prime Minister are you sure you don't want to come back in a couple of hours? Trent should be back soon".* Sabrina shakes her head asking, *"Liam can you please make me a cup of tea?".* Liam nods and heads to the kitchen while Sabrina checks her phone and thinks, *'I have a particularly good feeling that my daughter is near me'.*

Chapter 38

As Liam comes back with the tea and gives it to Sabrina, she thanks him as Callie and Trent come in. Callie is surprised to see the prime minister again while Trent had a sad look on his face; Callie turned to see Trent's sad expression asking, *"are you ok Trent?"*. Trent replies, *"I am ok, you go and unpack Angel."* Callie nods and leaves; Trent comes closer to Sabrina. He says, *"Sabrina, I thought we would have had this meeting in the evening."* Sabrina says, *"Trent I apologize for my unannounced arrival but hearing you had some update on Sophia's case made me feel optimistic"*. Trent looks at Liam and asks him to take the guards out; Sabrina worries and asks, *"Is everything ok?"*.

Trent tells her about Sophia's death as Sabrina drops the floor in shock; Trent closes his eyes and thinks, *'I am sorry for doing this, I can't lose my Angel.'* Sabrina gets up as she says, *"I always prayed and hoped my little girl would still be alive and safe; those monsters killed her"*. Trent apologises as Sabrina has one request and asks, *"I would like to meet Callie"*. Trent nods and shows her to Callie's room; Sabrina walks down the corridor and knocks on the door. Callie says, *"come in."* Callie was in deep thoughts over her family; Sabrina entered as Callie turned as Sabrina says, *"I am sorry to bother you sweetie, but I need your help"*. Callie noticed Sabrina's eyes were red and swollen because of crying. Sabrina explains Sophia's case to Callie who says, *"I am sorry for your loss. I lost my parents when I was younger and never met them"*. As Sabrina cries, Callie comes over and embraces her. Sabrina thinks, *'why does she feel so much like my little Sophia?'.* Sabrina says, *"I need your help please".* Callie asks, *"of course what can I help you with?".* Sabrina says, *"I would like my mother to meet you, I would like you to become my Sophia".*

Callie was stunned by the request as Sabrina says, *"please as a mother I am begging you."* After hearing about Scarlett's condition, Callie thinks for a moment and then nods agreeing to play the role. Sabrina hugs Callie and says, *"wherever your parents maybe I am sure they are proud of you."* Callie asks, *"where is your mom?".* Sabrina replies, *"Italy."* Callie says, *"I will speak to Trent about this, and I will see you soon."* Before Sabrina leaves, she gives a phone number and address. Callie watches Sabrina go and thinks, *'poor woman'.* Meanwhile, Seth is on a call and ends it saying, *"I love you too, son".* Storm comes into the office and Seth is shocked by his presence; Storm says, *"how dare you! you had someone try to kill Trent Reeves!".* Seth says, *"you haven't been doing your job."* Storm says, *"you could have killed me, but now you know what I quit".* Seth cocks his gun; Storm mentions Seth's son and he lets him go but not before threatening Seth. Alayna comes in and says, *"Boss what was all that about?".* Seth replies, *"nothing for you to worry about."* Later that evening Storm comes to meet Rick in the nightclub as they talk about things; Rick is stunned to hear that Storm is going to bring down the German Cartel Mafia. Storm says, *"I am not going to do this alone."* Trent comes into the room, looks at Storm and Rick saying, *"I am still in feeling rage after being told that you kissed my Angel, and this means death!".*

Chapter 39

As Rick was worried by Trent's words; Storm was cool and calm as he said, *"Trent you mean nothing to me! I don't bow or need to give you any loyalty and you know getting rid of me won't solve all your problems".* Trent notices Rick hiding behind the table scared. Storm rolls his eyes and introduces himself as his friend who is an expert hacker; As Trent and Storm talk; Storm says, *"Seth Romano has a son."* Trent was stunned to hear this and planned with Storm. Trent says, *"Once things are cleared and sorted; I need you to leave Storm."* Storm laughs asking, *"are you still feeling insecure that Callie will leave you? she chose you and let me tell you something, if you ever bring any tears or sadness in her eyes, I will kill you."* Rick jumped behind the table to hide; Trent looked at Storm with anger however assured him that Callie would always stay happy with him. As they talk things through; Rick comes out as Storm says, *"I need you to find the man."* Rick nods and says, *"I will get right on it".*

Meanwhile, Callie comes out of her room and sees Liam asking, *"Liam have you seen Trent? I haven't seen him since this morning."* Liam replies, *"Miss Callie, Trent has gone out on some urgent business. He should be back soon."* Callie gives a message to Liam and heads out; she comes back to her apartment, looks around and says, *"I've missed this place."* As she changed into her black PJs; she put Netflix on and watched, *'the Vampire diaries'.* Callie made some popcorn, she decided to give Hazel a call. Hazel was at the bakery eating doughnuts when

83

she saw Callie's call. Hazel answered sadly and Callie noticed her friend was still hurting after the breakup with Oliver. Hazel says, *"I gave him my heart and he broke it"*. Callie says, *"Haze you are strong, and you don't need a guy"*. Hazel and Callie talk who says, *"I need you to get in touch with the warden from the orphanage; she might be the only person to give me closure on my family"*. Hazel says, *"ok bestie I will get on that, I also wanted to tell you that I think you and Trent should be happy"*. Callie replies, *"what do you mean Haze? Do you think I should have sex with him?"*.

Callie had doubts however Hazel advises her saying, *"if you both love each other then why are you holding back? I know Trent loves you and you deserve happiness"*. Callie thanks Hazel ends the call and watches the series however still thinks of Hazel's words. Meanwhile, Trent comes home with flowers and calls out, *"Angel."* Liam says, *"Boss, Callie has gone back to her apartment."* Trent asks concerned, *"what do you mean she has gone back? Is everything ok?"*. Trent immediately heads out as Callie turns off the TV and she thinks about everything that has happened just as the doorbell rings. Callie wonders, *'who could that be?'*. As she opens to see Trent, he enters and asks, *"Angel why did you come back here?"*. Callie replied, *"I guess I thought you needed space after everything with Storm."* Trent pulls her closer and says *"Angel you are my breath and my heartbeat. I can't be apart from you"*. At that moment Callie pulled Trent and says, *"show me how much I mean to you. make me yours Trent"*. They kiss each other with passion; Trent stops asking, *"are you sure you want this Callie?"*.

Callie jumps on Trent and says, *"I want you to take me to the heavens."* Trent says, *"your wish is my command, Angel."* Callie rips Trent's shirt while Trent carries Callie to the bedroom still kissing passionately and he removes Callie's blouse. Trent kisses Callie all over as she moans Trent's name. Trent says, *"hearing you moan my name is sexy"*. Callie feels Trent's abdominal muscles as she kisses it; Trent and Callie continue the entire night to make love.

Chapter 40

The next morning: Callie is cuddled in Trent's arm; he awakes and watches her. He kisses her forehead as Callie awakes to Trent asking, *"morning my Angel how are you feeling?"*. Callie is hesitant before answering, *"Trent I was rubbish last night, wasn't I?"*. Trent asks, *"what do you mean?"*. Callie sighs and replies *"I am not experienced in you know..."*; Trent pulls her closer and says, *"you are my soulmate, my Angel and I love you."* As they kiss passionately, Callie says, *"Trent you have my body, heart, and soul!"*. Callie breaks the kiss and says, *"Trent I have to get to work."* Trent says, *"my Angel you are not leaving this bed today"*. Elsewhere, Hazel comes to the bakery and tidies up, she thinks about last night and tries to Callie. There is no response as Hazel says, *"I guess I will be managing the bakery today."* Hazel gets an incoming call from her phone from Aria who says, *"I have been trying to call Miss Callie, but I wanted to show the progress of the business"*. Hazel says, *"clever work Aria I will inform Callie."*

As the day goes by quickly; later that evening Storm comes to a bar where he sees Oliver in a state. Storm says, *"I thought I might find you here brother"*. Oliver was drunk and tells Storm about his breakup with Hazel. Storm says, *"I am sorry bro but maybe she was not the one."* Oliver says, *"don't talk about my Hazel like that, she's cute, sweet and I love her. if you didn't come between in falling for the wrong girl"*. Storm says, *"don't you dare turn this against me!"*. As they argue; Oliver blames Storm and says, *"you made me lie to my love"*. Storm snaps back at Oliver and says, *"you don't know anything and you blaming me isn't going to fix things";* As Storm explains his emotions, being a hitman and everything. Oliver begins to feel guilty while Storm walks out leaving him in deep thoughts.

Meanwhile, in Callie's apartment, she is preparing dinner for Trent and thinks of their love. Callie sees an incoming call from Hazel who is outside the bakery. Hazel asks, *"Callie where were you the entire day? I tried calling you and I have so much to tell you."* Callie tries to make an excuse however Hazel says, *"either you tell me where you were today, or I won't give you the information you asked for yesterday".* Callie tells Hazel she spent the night with Trent. Hazel says, *"congratulations my bestie is officially a woman."* Callie rolls her eyes asking, *"how was the business today?".* Hazel says, *"busy and Aria is doing an excellent job in Berlin."* As they talk; Trent comes to the kitchen and says, *"Angel come back to bed."* Hazel ends the call, walks over to her car, and is stunned to see Storm. Hazel asks stunned, *"what are you doing here?".* Storm tries to reason with Hazel and says, *"my intention was never to harm Callie!".* Hazel screamed at Storm and said, *"YOU'RE A MONSTER."* Storm comes closer saying, *"never call me that!".* Hazel grabs her phone warning Storm, *"if you don't leave now, I will call the police".* Storm says, *"the reason I am here to talk to you is because of my brother Oliver. He is suffering right now, and you are the only person that can help him".* Hazel thinks for a moment as Storm gives Hazel the location and says, *"thanks Hazel."* Hazel says, *"I am glad you have left Callie; she deserves real love, and they are officially together."* Storm asks, *"what do you mean officially together? Who's they?";* Hazel rolls her eyes, drives off as Storm thinks, *'no they cannot have.'* Storm soon had a cold and painful expression on his face.

Chapter 41

Elsewhere, Trent came into the kitchen and says, *"Angel I was calling you to the bed".* Callie says, *"I just finished preparing our dinner".* Trent says, *"I am hungrier for you."* Callie blushes as Trent lifts her on the kitchen table and whispers in her ears, *"I want to mark every corner of this house and make you mine".* As they kiss passionately Trent carries her to bed; Meanwhile Hazel comes to the bar as she sees Oliver drinking; Hazel walks up to him and says, *"Oliver".* Oliver says, *"maybe I am imagining you here".* Hazel comes over, pinches him as Oliver says, *"ouch."* Hazel tells Oliver that Storm found her and explained everything. Oliver drinks the glass and asks for another; Hazel stops him as he says, *"I love you so much but it's hurting me and Holden".* Hazel says, *"ever since we broke up my heart has been hurting too".* Oliver says, *"I need to tell you the truth about Holden".*

Hazel listens to Oliver's version, she feels sad and guilty; Hazel says, *"I called your brother a monster."* Oliver says, *"I am not mad at you babes".* Hazel turns to leave as Oliver pulls her hand as she turns to face him; their eyes meet and he says, *"I know you think I don't deserve your love, but you are important to me, and I can't lose you".* Hazel strokes his face, and they share a kiss while she says, *"you're important to me Oliver".* Oliver asks, *"can I have another chance?".* Hazel replies, *"first you need a shower".* Oliver pulls Hazel closer and kisses her passionately; As Hazel breaks the kiss she says, *"come on we need to go".* Hazel brings Oliver home as he heads into the shower; Hazel puts the TV on as

Oliver soon comes out without anything; Hazel turns her head and says, *"Oliver!"*. Oliver slips as Hazel holds him; however, Hazel hands him a towel and tells him to change. Hazel looks at her phone and then sends a message to Callie regarding the warden's address. The next morning Callie awoke to see Trent sleeping beside her as she smiles and blushed remembering their romantic night. As Callie got up to take a shower; Trent got into the bathroom as Callie felt shy about being naked with Trent. Trent says, *"Angel you don't need to be shy around me."* After a hot steamy shower Callie headed to the bakery while Trent left for his nightclub; elsewhere Hazel is with Oliver as they are asleep on the couch; Callie gets Hazel's message and says, *"I guess I better go and check this address out".* Soon, Callie comes to the address it is an old building as the woman says, *"I am sorry but the person you are looking for is the Italy Mental Asylum".* Callie thinks, *'maybe Trent can help me with this.'*

Later that afternoon as Callie comes home and freshens up; she is stunned to see Storm outside her apartment. Callie asks, *"Holden what are you doing here?".* Storm says, *"you gave him your virginity".* Callie tells Storm about her true feeling for Trent who says, *"I love you and I can't help this feeling towards you".* Callie apologises for punching him and encourages him to move on. Back in Trent's penthouse, he is talking with Liam about a proposal to Callie; Liam asks, *"did you tell Callie the truth about her family?".* Trent shakes her head and says, *"I won't let her past come between our future together".* Trent decides to give Callie her choice of the wedding; Liam has some doubts however the doorbell rings, and Trent open it asking surprised, *"Angel what are you doing here?".* Callie looks nervous replying, *"I need your help".* As Liam heads into the kitchen giving them space to talk; Callie talks about the warden from the orphanage and says, *"maybe she could give me the information I am looking for."* Trent asks, *"Callie are you sure you want to do this?"* Callie nods and tells Trent about the meeting with the Prime Minister a few days ago. Trent worries and then thinks, *'maybe the warden can be the key to helping me to stop Callie find out about the truth'.* Trent says, *"Angel leave it with me".* Storm comes to his place, packs his bags as Rick asks, *"Holden where are you going?".* Storm replies, *"I need to leave from here; too many memories."* Rick asks, *"what about the plan to bring down Seth Romano and his son?".* Storm says, *"Trent will help you and just keep me informed".* Rick tries to convince his friend to stay however Storm soon got a call for a new job.

Chapter 42

Rick asks Storm, *"what happened? Are you leaving?"*. Storm nods, back at Trent's penthouse he was speaking with Callie who was adamant to find out about her family, Callie says, *"Trent I just want closure"*. Trent hugs Callie and assures her he will sort things out; Callie gets a call from Hazel; Trent says, *"I am missing your sweet doughnuts and Frappuccino"*. Callie says, *"I can bring you some for the bakery"*. Trent pulls her closer, brings her to the kitchen as Callie bakes while Trent romances her as she finishes decorating; Trent says, *"we could enjoy these in my hot tub"*. Callie was stunned and asks, *"Mr. Reeves are you trying to seduce me?"*.

Trent says, *"we could do skinny-dipping."* Callie felt turned on as she smirked and blushes; a few hours later and Callie comes out as she grabs a towel, changes, and says, *"I'd better get to the bakery or Hazel will get worried"*. Later that evening Storm was in his apartment waiting for his Uber as a knock on the door surprised him; Oliver comes in and says, *"I can't believe you are doing this bro"*. Storm rolls his eyes as Oliver apologizes and says, *"I care for you and I'm sorry for arguing yesterday, I was drunk, and I said inconsiderate things"*. Storm says, *"I don't care if the entire world judges me, but I am your brother and I thought you had my back."* Oliver thanks Storm for bringing Hazel while Storm asks, *"are you back together?"*. Oliver replies, *"baby steps."* Storm and Oliver laugh as Oliver says, *"do you have to leave?"*. Storm says, *"I am sure a new surrounding will heal all my wounds and make me forget about Callie"*.

Oliver hugs Storm who gets a notification that his Uber has arrived. Trent was in his office as he called Liam over; Trent says, *"I have a plan to make sure Callie never finds the truth about her family."*

As Trent tells Liam about the warden and a secret plan; Liam is doubtful and says, *"Boss are you sure you don't want to tell Callie the truth?".* Trent gives a cold stare to Liam and says, *"I would rather die than her leaving me. I am her family, and I will protect her."* Liam sighs and says, *"a few days ago the prime minister welcomed Callie to her home in Italy?".* Trent sighs and says, *"let's just focus on dealing with the warden".* Liam asks, *"Boss should I prepare the jet?".* Trent replies, *"we are going on a train."* Liam goes and arranges the ticket; meanwhile Hazel is dealing with the last customers as Callie comes in and Hazel says, *"now you have finally come; business was busy today".* Hazel and Callie talk in the office; Hazel says, *"Oliver and I are giving our relationship a second chance. I might have misunderstood Holden."* Callie did not know how to feel when Storm was mentioned however Callie asks, *"did you tell Holden about me and Trent?".*

Hazel nods as Callie tells about Storm coming to see her; Hazel gets a call from Oliver who is upset while she asks, *"do you want me to come over?".* Hazel ends the call; Callie wonders in deep thoughts while Hazel informs her of Storm leaving. Hazel says, *"I need to go and check on Oliver".* Callie decides to do some baking; Meanwhile in a private mental facility in Sicily; Trent comes to see the warden who has become old and stares at Trent. Trent says, *"you are to help me or die understand!",* the woman looks shocked as Trent says, *"many years ago you took in a little girl without her family. Her name is Callie Dawson and I need you to tell her that her family is dead".* The warden says, *"if I do your work what will you give me?".* Trent asks, *"what would you like?".* The woman replies, *"money and freedom".* Trent agrees and says, *"I will bring her with me tomorrow."* Trent leaves with Liam as the warden sleeps; Meanwhile Seth is working on a plan as Alayna comes into the room and says, *"Boss I have some news to inform you."* Alayna tells Seth about Trent's plan to propose to Callie; Seth says, *"you know there is speculation of your engagement to Trent."* Seth whispers something to Alayna who says, *"it will be done, Boss."*

Chapter 43

Hazel is with Oliver on the couch who is in a sad mood, Hazel places her hand on his and says, *"Oliver you can talk to me"*. Oliver puts the TV on as Hazel heads to the kitchen to make some snacks; she soon comes back and asks, *"what movie are we going to watch?"*. Oliver replies, *"No Time to Die"*. As they watch the movie, Oliver places his hand on Hazel and thanks her for being there. Hazel and Oliver share a kiss as he says, *"I thought we were going do baby steps"*. Hazel laughs and kisses Oliver. The next day Trent comes in and thinks, *'I hope everything goes well today'*. Callie comes to the living room, sees Trent, and says, *"I missed you last night"*. Trent apologizes as he says, *"I had some business to attend to Angel however I have managed to get you access to see the warden"*. Callie is stunned and thanks Trent; Callie heads to change, Trent calls Liam to arrange for the train tickets. Liam says, *"Boss good luck."*

Back in Italy, Sabrina was in her office looking at a photo of Sophia as she reminisces the happy moments when a knock on the door interrupts her thoughts. Sabrina says, *"enter!"*. As Scarlett enters; Sabrina is stunned and says, *"doctors have advised you to rest mom"*. Scarlett asks, *"Sabrina do you have an update on Sophia's case? You told me a week ago you had some leads?"*. As Sabrina had a painful and sad pain in her eyes thinking, *'I am not going to hurt my mother more'*. Sabrina forces a smile and says, *"you're right mom I have some good news to tell you! I found Sophia and, in a few days, you will meet*

93

her." Scarlett had many questions and Sabrina answered them; she says, *"mom I need to keep this quiet as there could danger around".* Scarlett nods, hugs Sabrina and says, *"I cannot believe that after so many years I will be able hold my granddaughter in my arms."* Sabrina tells Scarlett more information as Scarlett says excitedly, *"I hope she can live with us."* Sabrina says, *"don't worry mom I will sort everything out."* Meanwhile Callie is on the train with Trent and asks, *"do you think the warden will have all my parent's information?".* Trent nods as Callie is nervous however Trent holds her hand and says, *"we still have a few hours before we reach how about we do something?".*

As Trent closes the door, he kisses Callie passionately as she sits on his lap, and they feel the passion and fire between them. Soon, they finally reach Italy; they head to the mental facility. Callie comes in as Trent sees the woman who says, *"Ah I recognise you little Callie Dawson."* Callie says, *"the reason for my visit is to find out about my parents."* The warden says, *"your parents died when you were six".* Callie says, *"I know but did you ever meet them or have any information about them?".* The Warden says, *"you parents probably hated you that's why they abandoned you; who would ever want to have kids? You were unloved and your parents killing themselves was purely out of guilt or maybe to save themselves".* Callie has tears in her eyes, runs out as Trent looks angrily at the Warden saying, *"you hurt my Angel."* Trent cocks his gun, he shoots her dead and then leaves; on the journey back home, Callie was in deep thoughts about everything. Trent tried to be comforting as they came home. Trent held her hand and says, *"Angel you haven't said anything the whole way back."* Callie says, *"I am tired."* Trent sees the pain in Callie's eyes saying, *"I am here for you always and forever."*

As Callie runs and hugs him, she says, *"I thought I would find out what happened to my parents."* Trent felt guilty hiding the secret and thought, *'I know you are in pain now, but I promise to give you happiness'.* Callie kisses Trent and says, *"you're my family and my world. I love you so much."* Trent says, *"I love you too my Angel."* Just then Callie's phone rings as she does not recognise the number however answers and is surprised to hear it is Sabrina. Sabrina asks, *"Callie sweetie how are you?"*. Callie wipes her tears, talks with Sabrina who says, *"I haven't heard from you in a while so I'm just checking in"*. As Sabrina and Callie talk, Trent looks at Callie and then heads to the kitchen to prepare dinner. Sabrina says, *"Callie you know from our conversation weeks ago, are you still up to come and see my mom and me?"*. Sabrina explained Scarlett's condition and her wish to meet her. Callie says, *"can we arrange it for the next few days?"*. Scarlett asks, *"would you like me to arrange any flights or anything?"*. Callie replies, *"don't worry I can manage it"*. Sabrina says, *"take care and see you soon."* Callie smelled something delicious as she saw Trent set up a candlelight dinner; Callie says, *"something smells delicious"*. Trent serves the pasta as Callie says, *"I will go freshen up."* As Callie comes back, she sits to eat as Trent asks, *"what was your call about?"*. Callie replies, *"Trent, the prime minister wants me to meet her mom, she lost her daughter."* Callie explained more; Trent listened and says, *"I think you should go to Italy but not tomorrow ok."* Callie takes a small amount on a fork as she says, *"I am not liking this pasta."* Callie gets up, she sits on Trent's lap as she says, *"feed me Trent."* Trent says, *"I thought you didn't like it Angel."* As Trent feeds her, she feeds him as she says, *"you have little bit of sauce on your lips"*. Callie kisses Trent who says, *"I don't need something sweet; you are my dessert"*. Trent carries her to the bedroom.

Chapter 44

The next morning Callie awoke, smiled as saw Trent sleeping next to her. Callie played with his hair as Trent says, *"Angel"*; As he opens his eyes and pulls Callie closer to him. Callie says, *"you said something will happen tonight".* Trent asks, *"don't I get my morning kiss?".* Callie replies, *"Trent are you hiding something from me?";* Trent sighs and says, *"you trust me, don't you? I have a special surprise for you tonight."* As they get out of bed; Trent goes for a shower while Callie calls Hazel. Hazel and Oliver are making out; Hazel sees Callie's call and says, *"hey Callie."* Callie says, *"Haze let's catch up at the bakery."* As they end the call; Oliver asks, *"babes do you have to go to work?".* Hazel nods and kisses him.

As Hazel is on the way to the bakery, she gets an incoming call from a private number. Trent says, *"hi Hazel, Trent here I have something special planned for Callie tonight and I need your help."* Hazel came to the bakery as Maisie says, *"Boss we need a dozen doughnuts and cupcakes".* Hazel gets some help to come as Callie comes in and sees the bakery busy. Hazel says, *"me and you are going out."* As they come to the shopping mall; Callie asks, *"Hazel what are we doing here?".* Hazel treats Callie to a girl's day out and has Callie's makeover done. Elsewhere, Trent is at the jewellers getting the ring as Alayna sees him. Trent hides the box in his jacket as Alayna says, *"hey babe!".* Trent rolls his eyes as he says, *"what do you want Alayna?".* Alayna says, *"I want us to be together."* Trent looks at her coldly and says, *"never."* As he leaves; Alayna watches him and makes a call to Seth to bring a plan forward.

As evening passes Callie comes home and sees a dress on her bed. Callie sees a note, *'to my sexy Angel wear this, I have a surprise for you'.* Callie changes as she comes downstairs to find an Uber is waiting for her. She comes to a decorated hotel, enters into the elevator, feeling a little nervous as the door opens to the rooftop with candles and petals. Callie smiles as she sees Trent in a tuxedo as he holds out his hand and says, *"Angel you look amazing".* As Callie takes Trent's hand, they look at the view of the city which sparkles as Callie says, *"this is so beautiful".* Trent wraps his arm around her waist; she feels Trent's breath on her neck as she says, *"I was scared, Trent."* Trent turns her around as he kisses her tears and says, *"you don't ever need to be scared Callie, I will always be by your side".* Callie and Trent share a passionate kiss as fireworks explode in the sky. Trent gets down on his knees as Callie smiles and he asks, *"Angel will you marry me?".* Callie nods happily as Trent puts the ring on Callie's finger, lifts her and kisses her passionately.

Soon, they come down to a suite decorated; Trent says, *"I want you now."* Callie kisses Trent as things get hot; The next morning Callie awakes and sees Trent has left a note. Callie comes to the penthouse; Liam congratulates her on the engagement as Liam and Callie talk; Liam asks, *"Callie you look nervous."* Callie says, *"I am ok."* Callie calls Sabrina to inform that she will be coming today as they end the call. Liam asks, *"do you need help in preparing the engagement party?".* Callie nods as she says, *"tell Trent that I am in Italy".* Meanwhile, Trent was in his office in the nightclub; he is stunned when Seth Romano comes to meet him. Trent asks, *"what the fuck do you think you are doing here?".* Seth pleads to join their Mafia together for more power as Trent laughs and says, *"my business here in Amsterdam is doing well and you are losing a lot".* Trent threatens Seth and says, *"leave Amsterdam".* Seth was stunned and shocked as he remembered his plan with Alayna saying, *"you will pay and suffer for this Trent Reeves!".* As Seth left; Trent called

Rick to meet, and he came to his nightclub. Trent asks, *"what is the update on Seth's son?"*. Rick lets Trent know what is happening as Trent asks, *"where is Storm?"*. Rick says, *"he has left Amsterdam for a new job"*. Trent nods, leaves but not before inviting Rick to his engagement party with Callie in a few days.

Chapter 45

As Rick called Storm; he asked, *"how are you?"*. Storm says, *"I am in London, everything is okay. What is up with Seth's son?"*. Rick gives him an update on Oliver and the case; he is feeling a bit tense as Storm says, *"Rick just say what you want to say!"*. Rick mentions Callie's engagement to Trent; Storm felt anger as Rick says, *"bro it's better you move on."* Storm ends the call, thinks of Callie, and gets tears in his eyes; Meanwhile Callie has almost reached Sicily and is picked up by a private car; In the office, Sabrina and Scarlett are talking; Sabrina says, *"mom please don't overwhelm her!"*. Scarlett says, *"I can't wait to meet her."* Just then there is a knock on the door as Sabrina says, *"enter!"*. As Callie comes in, she sees Sabrina and the elderly woman; Scarlett comes to her and says, *"it's you, my little Sophia grew up"*.

Sabrina wiped a tear from her eyes as Callie did not know why but hugged Scarlett, she felt a strange feeling in her heart. Scarlett says, *"I have so much to talk with you sweetie and so much to show you."* Sabrina says, *"mom I think Callie is tired and needs to rest after a long journey."* Sabrina shows Callie to her room; Scarlett sighs as she soon leaves and knocks on Callie's door who opens and says, *"come with me dear."* Callie came into Scarlett's room they talked for hours; Callie mentioned Trey as Scarlett noticed a ring on her finger and asks, *"are you married dear?"*. Callie says, *"I am only engaged but I would love for you to come to my engagement and wedding"*. Scarlett asks, *"have you set a date?"*. Callie says, *"I will have the engagement party this weekend and wedding in a few weeks".* As Scarlett says, *"I will tell the good news to Sabrina".* Callie notices Scarlett feeling unwell, helps her as Scarlett says, *"it's ok I will be fine you take a rest."* Sabrina was in the office talking with Nathan about what to do; Sabrina says, *"I am still reeling from finding out my daughter is no more in this world".* Nathan gives some advice however both are unaware; Scarlett has overheard the conversation. Scarlett says, *"I have a strong feeling that Sophia is Callie; I just need to bring the truth out."*

Scarlett heads down the corridor thinking of a plan. Later that evening back in Amsterdam; Trent misses Callie as Liam comes and says, *"Boss we need to talk."* As they talk about the upcoming engagement party; later that evening, Callie walks around the mansion and she comes across a photo of a young girl wearing a locket. Callie notices it and wonders, *'where have I seen that locket?'.* Just then Sabrina comes behind her as Callie turns spooked; Sabrina says, *"sorry sweetie are you ok?".* Callie sighs and nods as Scarlett comes there and says, *"there you are Callie dear."* Callie says, *"sorry I wandered off, I was trying to find Scarlett".* Sabrina says, *"you must be hungry.",* as they eat lasagne; Sabrina asks, *"Is everything ok?".* Callie informs Sabrina of her engagement party as Sabrina congratulates her. Scarlett says, *"I can't wait to see my beautiful granddaughter. And a beautiful wedding."* As Sabrina called one of her staff to bring back Scarlett to her room. Sabrina and Callie had a talk; Callie tells her about her family. As Sabrina gets up crying; Callie comes over to her and hugs her as Callie wonders, *'why am I feeling a strong pain in my heart? This woman does not deserve pain.'* Sabrina assures Callie she will always be there for her. Sabrina thinks, *'how I wish my daughter could have been you.'* As everyone soon heads to bed; Callie speaks to Trent as she soon falls asleep. Trent hears Callie snoring as he says, *"goodnight Angel!".*

Chapter 46

The next few days pass quickly; Scarlett develops a bond with Callie while Sabrina captures the memories; Callie gets a call from Hazel regarding the bakery and tells her, *"I will be back tomorrow"*. As Callie comes to the kitchen, she puts an apron on and bakes cupcakes and doughnuts; she brings it into the dining room; Scarlett and Sabrina come in and smelt the aroma of the bakes. Callie says, *"I have prepared a treat before I leave."* Scarlett takes a doughnut, eats it, and says, *"this is delicious Sophia"*. Sabrina takes a bite of the cupcake; she enjoys it as Callie looks at Sabrina who gives her a smile. Soon, Callie packs her bag to leave for her flight; Sabrina comes and hugs her and says, *"I will see at your engagement party."* Callie nods and leaves; Scarlett sees Callie leaving and thinks, *'I have no doubt in my mind; you are our Sophia'*. The next morning Callie comes home as Trent is sleeping; Callie comes and cuddles herself in his arms as Trent awakes and says, *"Angel you are back."* Callie kisses Trent and says, *"I missed you."* Trent kisses her as they soon fall asleep; later that afternoon Callie comes to see Hazel at the bakery; Hazel updates on her what has been happening. Callie says, *"forget a minute about business. We need to go shopping."* As they head out to the shop; Hazel and Callie spend hours shopping as Trent comes to his nightclub; he sees Alayna in a skimpy outfit. Alayna tries to seduce him however Trent orders his men to get rid of her. Callie says, *"I can't believe my engagement party is tomorrow and, in a few weeks, I will be Mrs. Reeves"*. Hazel is happy for her friend and asks, *"did you manage to get information from the warden on your parents?"*. Callie shakes her head and tells Hazel about Sabrina and Scarlett. Hazel says, *"wow so much has happened in your life."* As the two friends hug and leave, Seth meets Alayna and says, *"I will be moving to Italy."* Alayna asked shocked, *"what do you mean moving?"*.

Seth tells her about his meeting with Trent. Alayna says, *"Trent needs to pay."* Seth packed up as he told Alayna to try and break his engagement with Callie. Alayna nods, *"yes Boss";* later that evening Trent was in the hot tub waiting for Callie as she came in and he held her in his arms; Callie says, *"Trent I have the sexiest outfit for our engagement party."* Trent says, *"Angel you will be wonderful in any outfits."* As they kiss; Trent gets a call from Liam regarding some files and says, *"keep it in the safe."* Trent pulls Callie out, kisses her passionately and soon takes her to bed. As Callie sleeps, she has a dream about the locket and wonders, *'where have I seen it?'.* The day before the engagement; Callie comes to her apartment, looks around and then opens a safe at the bottom of her wardrobe however she forgot the code. Callie sighs and says, *"I'd better go meet Hazel."* Elsewhere, Sabrina was with the doctor who was examining Scarlett; Sabrina asked, *"how is she, doctor? Will my mom be able to come with me to Amsterdam?"*. The doctor says, *"she is ok to travel."* Scarlett says, *"I am not going to miss my granddaughter's engagement for the world".* Back in London, Storm was training in a room, thought of Callie and remembered their moments; when a call came in from Rick and tells him, *"I will be leaving tonight."* As the morning came for the engagement; Callie awoke in Trent's arms filled with worries and doubt however Trent kissed Callie and said, *"the world will know you are my Angel."* As they kiss passionately; Callie phone rings as Trent asks, *"do not worry about the call. How about you join me for a shower and then breakfast?"*

Chapter 47

Callie says, *"Trent I have so much to do today"*. Trent heads into the shower as Callie checks her call and sees it was Sabrina's call. She calls Sabrina who says, *"hi sweetie how are you?"*. Callie replies, *"I am ok Sabrina, how are you and Scarlett?"*. Scarlett takes the phone and says, *"sweetie how are you? I am so excited today for your party"*. Callie laughs and soon hears Trent calling her name. Callie says, *"I will speak to you soon"*. As Callie comes to the kitchen; she is stunned to see Trent naked in a chef apron as he says, *"breakfast with a twist."* Callie laughs, takes a piece of strawberry, is about to feed Trent but eats it. Trent lifts her, tickles her as Callie looks at the time and says, *"Trent I have some things to sort out for tonight."* Callie asks, *"Trent do you know where the party will be?"*. Trent nods asking, *"do you remember the party at my place? Well on the bottom floor there is a big hall."* Callie heads to get change, meets with Hazel and bakes some cakes and doughnuts. Hazel says, *"you are not going to bake your wedding cake."* Callie asks, *"why not? I make the best cakes."*

Hazel rolls her eyes replying, *"tonight is your engagement, and I don't want you to be stressed out"*. Hazel tells Maisie to manage the bakery while she takes Callie to get a pedicure and facial treatment; as they eat lunch; Callie says, *"you know about mine and Trent's relationship, but I haven't asked how you and Oliver have been?"*. Hazel says, *"he is such a softie and I love him"*. Storm came to his apartment as he saw Rick and asked, *"why did you call me back?"*. Just then Oliver comes and hugs Storm; he says, *"bro I missed you."* Storm sighs and says, *"let's catch up over a drink."* He heads for a shower; Rick and Oliver look at each other while Rick asks, *"will you be able to bring him to the party tonight?".* Oliver nods and says, *"yes this is the only way he will be able to move on".* Meanwhile, Scarlett was resting in her room and felt a little weak however Sabrina came and checked on her mom as the evening approached Callie felt excited and so many emotions. Elsewhere, Trent was getting ready in his room. Liam came and said, *"you look dapper Boss."* As Callie came down, she saw a limo outside, came in and saw Hazel as they hugged. Hazel says, *"you look amazing."*

Callie blushes and they soon come to the party; Oliver is with Rick while Storm comes out in a suit and wonders, *'where are these two taking me?'.* At the party, Callie looks around nervously as Trent sees her, comes over to her and says, *"Angel you look gorgeous".* Sabrina and Scarlett come in; Callie welcomes them as Trent says, *"it's a pleasure for you to join us, Sabrina".* Scarlett says to Callie, *"you look so beautiful".* Callie smiles as Hazel goes to make a call; Rick, Storm, and Oliver come to the party who asks, *"why have you brought me here?".* Rick and Oliver head in as Storm follows them; Callie and Trent head upstairs to a room as Callie looks in the mirror while Trent comes behind her and kisses her neck. Trent says, *"Angel I want to ravish you right now".* Callie laughs and says, *"Trent we need to get back to the party".* Trent takes her hand and they both leave.

Chapter 48

A s Storm looks around, he heads to the bar as Hazel sees Storm and turns to Oliver. Hazel asks, *"babes what is Holden doing here?"*. Oliver says, *"Rick and I had a plan for him to meet Callie and move on"*. Sabrina comes over to meet Hazel, Rick, and Oliver; Hazel recognizes Sabrina and says, *"what an honor to meet you Miss Prime Minister"*. Oliver asks, *"Prime Minister? Of which country?"*. Sabrina replies, *"Italy and it's nice to meet Callie's friends"*. A few moments later, Scarlett comes, she fakes feeling dizzy as Liam comes over while Sabrina worries over Scarlett; Liam says, *"Sabrina I can take your mother to Callie's apartment which is a few minutes away from here."* Scarlett takes Liam's hand just as Sabrina asks, *"mom are you sure you will be, ok?"*.

Scarlett nods, takes Liam's arm and leaves; just then the lights go off as a spotlight shine on Trent and Callie coming down the stairs; As Storm is drinking at the bar; he soon notices a crowd gathered, Trent makes a speech and has a dance with Callie. As the music plays, Callie smiles at Trent who spins her however, she loses her balance, and is about to fall when someone catches her; Callie opens her eyes and is stunned to see Storm holding her. As the lights come on; Trent is not happy to see Storm; Callie asks, *"Holden what are you doing here?"*. Storm replies, *"firefly is this your party?"* Trent comes over, holds Storm's collar and both argue; Oliver and Rick come in between as Callie goes out. As Callie waits outside thinking, *'why can't Trent control his issues?'*. Just then Trent lets Storm go and looks for Callie; Alayna comes in front of Callie and says, *"nice dress."* Alayna says, *"we never got to meet officially the other day. I'm Alayna Trent's ex-fiancée."* Callie laughs and says, *"good joke."*

Alayna shows Callie some intimate photos of her and Trent; Callie looks shocked as Trent comes out. He yells at Alayna who rolls her eyes and leaves; Callie looks at Trent who says, *"Angel come back inside."* Callie comes inside but runs upstairs as Hazel notices this; Callie says, *"how could you Trent? I trusted you and you...".* Trent comes closer to her as she asks, *"how could you hurt me like this?".* Trent says, *"Angel she means nothing to me."* Callie says, *"Trent I need some space."* She leaves as Storm is in the flower garden smoking when Rick comes and talks to him. Storm says, *"I can't believe you brought me back."* Rick says, *"I just wanted you to get closure.";* Rick says, *"I also have something to discuss with you about Trent".* Soon, Trent announces the party is finishing; Kaitlyn and Matthew come over as they say, *"we look forward to the wedding."* Daphne and Liam also congratulate Trent who sighs. Callie comes downstairs trying to look for Hazel but bumps into Sabrina. Sabrina notices Callie is upset, been crying and she says, *"I feel so lost".* Sabrina asks, *"did Trent hurt you?".* Callie cries without responding, Sabrina hugs her while Callie feels peace in her arms. Back in Callie's apartment, Liam is looking after Scarlett as he gets a call from Trent. Scarlett says, *"you better go, I will be ok."* Liam asks, *"are you sure?".*

Scarlett nods and Liam leaves; Scarlett looks around and then comes into Callie's room and the bathroom as she takes her toothbrush and a hair comb. Scarlett says, *"I will reunite my daughter and granddaughter; in my heart, I know that Callie is Sophia".* Back in the park, Storm noticed Rick being hesitant and says, *"Rick just tell me."* Rick explains Trent's secret mission back in Italy, Storm listens however is stunned when Rick says, *"Callie is the missing daughter of the Italian Prime Minister."* Storm laughs and says, *"you're having a laugh".* Rick had a serious expression on his face as Storm says, *"we need to tell Callie the truth."* Rick says, *"we don't have any lead at the moment, but I will update you on this."* Storm gets a call and says, *"I need to head back to London."*

Chapter 49

As Sabrina and Callie talk, Sabrina says, *"Callie, you know you can come and stay with me and my mom if you want to get away for a few days."* Callie says, *"I don't want to be a burden."* Sabrina says, *"you are never a burden, you are a blessing."* Callie nods and says, *"let's head to my place."* As they leave; Scarlett sends off the DNA sample however begins to feel dizzy and collapses on the bed; Liam comes to the party to find it is empty as Trent has been pacing anxiously; Liam asks, *"Boss what happened?".* Trent tells about Alayna and Storm while Liam says, *"so much happened? Where's Callie?".* Trent tries to call Callie however it goes to voicemail. Liam asks, *"Boss are you sure you still want to hide the truth about Callie's family from her? I mean you never told her about Alayna and...".* Trent says, *"I can't lose my Angel."*

Meanwhile, Rick is at the airport with Storm who is about to go in his flight; he gets a call from Trent asking, *"have you heard from Callie?".* Rick replies, *"no";* Trent has a doubt that Storm is involved however Rick says, *"Holden is flying out now".* As the call gets disconnected; Storm wonders, *'what is going on?'.* Rick mentions Callie's disappearance as Storm gets protective however Rick gives Storm a reality check and says, *"you head to London, I will try to find a clue for someone who knows Callie's true identity".*

Storm nods and leaves to fly to London; Meanwhile, both Liam and Trent are thinking; Liam asks, *"Boss I have a question to ask about Ellis. What did you do to her?".* Trent says, *"she is fine and is in Spain;*

focus we need to find Callie." Liam nods and says, *"CCTV."* They head to the camera room to try and find Callie's location; meanwhile, Callie comes to her place, finds it is quiet and comes into her room to find Scarlett asleep. Callie comes and gently says, *"Scarlett come on, time to go".* Scarlett does not awake; Callie panics and screams, *"SABRINA!".*

Sabrina comes running in while Callie cries over Scarlett; Sabrina checks her mother's pulse and says, *"call an ambulance now!".* Elsewhere, Trent and Liam are still searching; Trent gets a call as he is shocked and says, *"I'll be on my way."* Liam asks, *"Boss what happened?".* Trent says, *"I'll explain on the way."* Soon, Callie and Sabrina wait outside the hospital room; Nate is closely guarding the corridor. Sabrina cries and says, *"I can't let her leave me. she's all I have."* Callie hugs Sabrina and assures her that everything will be ok; Nate comes and says, *"Madam, Trent Reeves is requesting permission to come?"*; Callie feels doubtful, looks at Sabrina who understands and tells Nate, *"Send him up".* Trent runs to Callie who cries in his arm. Sabrina gives them space and goes to look for the doctor; Callie says, *"time is so precious, and we have to make each moment count."* Trent looks at Callie who closes her eyes, extends her hand to Trent saying, *"if you look me into my eyes and promise me you will not lie or deceit me for anything then we can move past Alayna."* Trent takes Callie's hand and kisses it as he promises and hugs her; however, hides his sad look on his face. Soon, Sabrina comes back and says, *"Callie I can't move my mom back to Italy as she is now on the life support machine."* Trent asks, *"is there anything we can do?".* Sabrina replies, *"we are just going have to give it time."* Callie hugs Sabrina she assures that Trent and she will beside her for support; days turn into weeks as Scarlett's condition deteriorates.

Callie has been so busy with wedding planning with Hazel and managing the bakery that she found herself exhausted. Hazel gives Callie a glass of water asking, *"are you ok?".* Callie nods as she gets a call from Sabrina to come to the hospital; Hazel says, *"you go, and I will manage here".* Callie calls Trent to the hospital, Sabrina is outside the room just as the doctor comes. Callie asks, *"what happened?"*. The doctor apologizes for the loss of Scarlett Anderson. Sabrina cries while Callie hugs her; Sabrina says, *"my mom, she left me. my daughter's death and now my mom is too"*. As Trent watches them, he comes over to Sabrina saying, *"you don't have to feel alone or like a stranger; we will always be with you."* Sabrina arranges for Scarlett's body to be flown back to Italy for the funeral.

Meanwhile, Seth is talking with Alayna about a new plan to bring down Trent Reeves. Storm finishes his job in London, calls Rick and asks, *"do you have any update on the lead for Callie's case?"*. Rick replies, *"better you come back, and we talk about this."* As Trent stays with Callie in Sabrina's house; he looks around at the photos and sees Callie wearing the necklace, thinking, *'why does this necklace look so familiar?'*. Soon the funeral arrangement is done; Sabrina comes wearing a black dress and gives a white tulip to Callie who asks, *"are you ready for this?"*. Sabrina replies, *"I don't think I can do this."*

Chapter 50

C allie takes Sabrina's hand and says, *"you don't have to go through this alone. I will be with you every step of the way."* Sabrina cries as Callie says, *"let's go."* They come to the church; Sabrina says a few words as Callie takes the stage and gives a heartfelt speech. At the graveyard, Sabrina puts the white tulip on the grave and says, *"rest in peace mom. I love you always and forever."* Callie puts the white tulip and says, *"we may have known each other for a short while but you will live on in our memory".* Trent puts a flower on as he thinks, *'I am sorry for your death. But I promise to give Callie the best future and life'.* Sabrina cries, Callie looks at Trent and says, *"I think we should postpone our wedding".* Sabrina says, *"no sweetie, you deserve your special day, and I am sure my mom would have wanted it too. I do have a request though".* Callie says, *"of course Sabrina what is it?".* Sabrina speaks with Callie privately; she nods and comes back to Trent. Trent asks, *"what is it, Angel?".* Callie asks, *"can we have our wedding here?".* Trent says, *"whatever you wish for."*

Trent happily kisses Callie, and they share a hug. Meanwhile Rick is at his secret base trying to locate someone from the records; Storm soon comes asking, *"any update on the case?"* Rick says, *"I don't have any leads yet."* In Spain, Ellis was carrying the shopping as she thought of Sophia while Rick's computer located Ellis; Rick says, *"Storm you need to head over to Spain".* As final preparations were done; Trent invited over some Mafia families to join and also made sure security was doubled. In Spain, Storm came to an old house and rang the bell.

Ellis opened as Storm says, *"you know about Callie, I mean Sophia?"*. Ellis tried to pretend she did not and said, *"please spare my life. I told the truth about Sophia to Trent"*. As she runs onto the road scared, an oncoming car hits her; Storm comes over to her, holds her and says, *"you'll be ok. Look I am not here to hurt you."* Storm's phone rings, he answers as Ellis is badly injured and heavily bleeding as she says, *"before I die, I want to tell you that Sophia is the six-year-old girl who was taken from her family; Whatever name she has now she is the Italian prime minister's daughter"*. Ellis dies as Storm closes her eyes; he calls the ambulance and leaves from there; Storm says, *"you have the recording saved; tomorrow we tell the truth to Callie."*

Meanwhile, Callie is with Sabrina baking in the kitchen, Sabrina says, *"I don't really bake much"*. Callie sees Sabrina's cake saying, *"I am sure decorating will be better."* As Sabrina wipes a tear from her eyes; Callie asks, *"I don't have my family to be with me tomorrow for my special day, but can you give me away?"*. Sabrina hugs, kisses Callie's forehead and nods. As Storm takes the flight to reach home; Callie and Trent both fall asleep thinking of each other. The next day is the wedding, as Sabrina is in her office sorting out the mails and posts when a letter captures her attention. Callie is with Hazel who says, *"Callie I am so happy for your special day."* Hazel gives her a makeover; Callie does not know why but she feels nauseous, runs to the bathroom, and soon comes out; Hazel asks, *"are you ok bestie?"*; Callie nods and replies, *"maybe it is just nerves."* Trent is with Liam and are getting ready as Liam gets a phone call about Ellis; Trent sees Liam's worried expression. Liam says, *"Ellis is dead Boss!"*. Trent sighs and says, *"we have a wedding to go to"*. Elsewhere, Nate knocks on the door of Sabrina's office; Sabrina says, *"enter!"*. Nate asks, *"madam, are you ready for the wedding?"*. Sabrina says, *"give me a sec."* Sabrina opens, reads, and then drops the letter in shock.

Chapter 51

Elsewhere, Callie fixed herself, Hazel says, *"let's take a selfie."* After Callie came to look for Sabrina; Sabrina took the letter as Callie found her in the office. Sabrina says, *"Callie sweetie I have something to tell you".* As Oliver, Rick and Storm come into the office; Hazel asks, *"babes what are you doing here?".* Callie looks worried and asks, *"is everything ok?".* Rick plays the recording of Ellis while Callie is confused just as Sabrina shows the letter. Callie reads it while Sabrina says, *"you're my missing daughter; Sophia."* Sabrina has tears in her eyes as Callie holds Sabrina's hand and calls her mom. Sabrina kisses Callie's cheeks and hands saying, *"my beautiful baby girl."* Storm says, *"I am sorry Callie, but Trent lied to you."* Callie's sadness soon turned into anger saying, *"mom, Holden, Oliver, Rick, and Hazel. I want you all to be at my wedding."* Sabrina says, *"I am going to end him".*

At the venue, Trent looked at the guests as Hunter came over and congratulated Trent, and Matthew, and Kaitlyn, Daphne, and Liam also congratulated him. Trent looked at the time and wondered, *'where is Angel?'.* As the music begins; Sabrina holds Callie's arm and brings her to the altar as Hazel, Rick, Oliver, and Storm come. Callie looks at Trent who smiles at her saying, *"Angel you look so beautiful".* The priest says, *"we are gathered to join these two people Trent and Callie in holy matrimony."* As they each say their vows; Callie sees Trent in her eyes smiling and remembers words of honesty; Callie pushes Trent and says, *"NO!".* Trent asks, *"Angel are you ok?";* As the guests wonder, *'what is happening?'* Callie has tears in her eyes saying, *"I can't believe you betrayed me in such a way."* Trent asks, *"what are you talking about?".* Callie says, *"how about the truth that my mom is alive?".* Trent tries to console her as she says, *"I gave you a chance, I told you I only wanted honesty, but you broke my trust and lied once again."* As tears ran down Callie's eyes; Trent felt her sadness saying, *"I only wanted to protect you."* Callie laughs and says, *"protect me? what a joke! You're a selfish jerk!".*

Callie pushes Trent runs down the altar as Sabrina goes after her. Callie removes her veil and says, *"mom we need to get back to Amsterdam."* As they fly back; Storm comes to Trent who holds his collar angrily, *"you are responsible for this."* Storm pushes, punches Trent and says, *"you don't deserve Callie's love".* In the plane, Sabrina sat down with Callie who was in a state of shock while Sabrina hugged Callie. Sabrina angrily says, *"I will end him! I will make him suffer."* Callie says, *"mom, I have a plan which is why we are heading back to Amsterdam".* In a private base, Seth is with Alayna just then there is a knock on the door. Seth says, *"enter!".* Nate and another guy come in; Kevin says, *"hello dad."* Alayna hugs Kevin happily saying, *"bro."* Nate gives the news of Trent's marriage breaking as Seth says, *"we need to formulate a plan."* Nate says, *"I also have to inform you that the prime minister's child is found. She has a daughter which is Callie Dawson."* Kevin thinks and says, *"I have a plan and Nate you will be an immense help in this."* Seth asks, *"what is the plan?".* Kevin says, *"you want to trap Trent, and what best way than to frame him for the beloved Prime minister's death.".* Alayna says, *"truly diabolical brother."* Kevin says, *"dad you know what my goal is to become the PM and gain power and you will have your revenge over Trent."* They all laughed evilly and discuss a secret plan to move forward. Elsewhere, Liam and Trent have left the venue as Liam sees Trent is broken. Trent says, *"my Angel... she hates me.... I......".* He cries while Liam holds him; Trent's phone rings and he answers to find out that Callie has left the country; Trent worries and says, *"maybe she has gone home".* Liam get the jet ready to head back to Amsterdam."

Chapter 52

On the flight back to Amsterdam, things were quiet as Callie had a plan in her mind; Sabrina says, *"sweetie I want to take you away from all this; somewhere quiet."* Callie says, *"I know mom, but this is important".* Callie calls Hazel saying, *"I need you to do something for me."* Hazel nods as Callie tells her a plan, despite Hazel's objection Callie manages to convince her friend. They finally reach Amsterdam; Sabrina asks, *"do you need my help?".* Callie replies, *"mom just wait for me at the hotel."* Callie wears a black mask around her face, comes into Trent's nightclub and remembers when Liam and Trent had a private conversation; she sneaks into the back and comes to the office as she looks around and sees a big photo frame of Trent with an older man.

Callie lifts the frame to reveal a safe and thinks, *'what could the code be?'.* Callie thinks for a moment, types in her birthday and it opens; Back in the hotel; Sabrina hears a knock on the door, opens and is stunned to see Nate. As Trent and Liam come to Amsterdam; Trent gets a call from Hazel to meet. Meanwhile, Callie takes some of the files into a brown envelope, she closes the safe puts the frame back and sneaks out. Trent sees Hazel asking, *"how is my Angel?";* Hazel replies, *"you shouldn't worry about her because you have caused her pain."* Trent tries to explain however Hazel says, *"I wish you had never come back into Callie's life."*

As Trent leaves, Liam calls from the penthouse and says, *"Boss she is not here."* Trent thinks for a moment and heads over to Callie's apartment. Callie packs a few things, she comes back to the wardrobe safe and types in a code as it opens; Callie removes the velvet cloth to reveal the locket; however, just then she hears noises in the living room; Callie wipes a tear and comes out. Trent says, *"Angel please listen to me."* Callie says, *"why should I? so you can tell me more lies."* Trent says, *"I know what I did was wrong but I..."*; Callie says, *"remember when you told me about Leone and how much he meant you; I would have done anything to find a family; my mom, grandmother, and despite the fact you knew the truth. You hid it all and betrayed my trust."* Trent drops to his knees begging Callie for another chance and forgiveness; Callie says, *"I want you to see to something."* Trent looks at Callie who brings her veil from her dress as she gets a match and lights it. It begins to burn while Trent attempts to put it out; Callie coldly says, *"just like this fire has burned the veil, it is what you have done to me Trent; you've burned my trust, dream, and our future."* Trent apologizes as Callie looks at him with hatred and anger in her eyes and says, *"you don't deserve me, my love, or anything."* Callie walks out of her apartment, Trent cries and screams Callie's name in pain.

Meanwhile, Sabrina and Nate talk, Nate says, *"madam your image and reputation is hanging by a thread."* Sabrina says, *"my first priority is my daughter."* Sabrina gets a call from Callie regarding evidence and documents regarding Trent's businesses before ending the call. Sabrina tells Nate about bringing Trent's downfall. Nate listens and says, *"I will arrange for the conference in a few days in Italy madam."* Soon, Callie comes to the hotel; Nate comes out as he makes a call to Kevin informing of Sabrina's plan. Kevin laughs and says, *"this is good... it will make our job much easier."* Kevin gives further instructions to Nate and says, *"don't forget to keep me posted."* Nate nods and says, *"yes sir."*

Chapter 53

Callie gives the brown envelope to Sabrina; Sabrina notices Callie's sadness and asks, *"mom is there somewhere we can go together away from everything?"*. Sabrina hugs Callie and nods replying, *"I have a small house in Santorini, Greece"*. Callie phones Hazel who is with Oliver; Callie asks, *"can you come with me to Santorini?"*. As Sabrina makes sure Callie is packed with her luggage; they drive to the airport; Sabrina says, *"sweetie I need to get this file over to security and also I have a conference in a few days in Italy."* Callie asks, *"mom will you not come with me?"*. Callie opens her bag and shows the locket to Sabrina; Sabrina says, *"you had this with you for so many years, you know it belonged to Scarlett"*. Sabrina opens the locket to reveal a picture of her and a man. Callie asks, *"is that my dad?"*. Sabrina nods, wipes a tear, and makes Callie wear the locket. Hazel comes with Oliver as Hazel runs to Callie and hugs her; Sabrina says, *"I will be back soon."* As the plane takes off; Callie sees her mom waving through the window.

Sabrina makes a call to Storm and says, *"I need you to take care of my daughter, she is on her way to Santorini."* Storm nods saying, *"yes Madam I will be on the first flight out."* Liam comes to Callie's apartment and sees Trent's state who says, *"my Callie... my Angel."* Liam says, *"Boss all is not lost; please pull yourself together."* Meanwhile. Sabrina heads back to Italy in the office; she thinks of Callie, makes a call, and then leaves. Elsewhere Hazel, Oliver, and Callie land in Greece; it is beautiful with the sound of waves and beautiful surroundings. Callie thinks of Trent however Hazel says, *"I will make something for us to eat"*. Callie takes some rest as she does not know why but she feels nauseous and gets sick in the bathroom. A few hours later; Sabrina comes to Santorini, opens the door and Callie says, *"mom you came."* Sabrina says, *"sweetie we were apart for so many years, I couldn't abandon you now not when you need me the most."* Hazel comes into the living room with Chinese noodles and dumplings; Callie does not know why but the smell of greasy food is making her sick. Sabrina notices this and asks Callie, *"are you, ok Sweetie? You look pale! Should I call the doctor?"*. Callie heads to her room to rest; The next few days pass, Callie slowly heals from her broken heart and also forms a stronger bond with her mom.

Meanwhile back in Amsterdam, Trent is heartbroken as Liam tries to help him however Trent says, *"I am not going back to Spain without Callie and as for my business I don't care."* Liam says, *"Boss there's something I need to tell you about Callie."* As Liam mentions the nightclub break-in; Trent thinks, *'my Angel would never betray me.'* As Sabrina flies back to Italy for the conference; Hazel and Callie are watching a movie on the TV when the doorbell rings and Oliver open to see it is Storm. Oliver says surprised, *"Bro what are you doing here?"*. Storm comes in and sees Hazel and Callie; he gives Callie a smile and asks, *"firefly how are you feeling?"*. Callie heads to her room and closes the door. Hazel says, *"Holden it's not you, she has just been really sad."* Back in Italy, Sabrina is almost ready to do the conference for tomorrow when she gets a call from security regarding the evidence against Trent Reeves. Sabrina says, *"thank you for your help, I will take it from here."* Later that evening; Hazel comes to Callie's room asking, *"Callie you need to get some fresh air; why don't you join me and Oliver on the beach?"* Callie feels herself and looks in the mirror as she asks Hazel, *"do I look fatter to you?"*. Oliver calls Hazel who says, *"hang on babes."* Hazel says, *"Callie you are beautiful and sexy! Never forget that!"*. Callie smiles saying, *"Haze you go and have fun, I will head out maybe later on"*.

Chapter 54

S abrina was getting ready for her conference, took a deep breath and came out of her office outside when a group of reporters and journalists were waiting for her. Sabrina came to the podium and stood; she said, *"Welcome everyone and thank you for being available to come to this conference. I have two things I would like to address..."* first, she briefly mentions Callie; her voice becomes firm and says, *"I would like to mention about Mafia dealings in Italy and over Europe, leaders are kept quiet by bribes or corruption; but I announce that all Mafia Associations will be destroyed; but further to this I will be working with security, agents and special forces to bring down all Mafia Bosses."* As the media takes her photo she says, *"One Mafia Cartel, in particular, Black Panther: the leader Trent Reeves".*

The media soon had many questions for Sabrina, she answers them confidently. Liam and Trent are on their way to the conference while Liam asks, *"Boss do you really want to do this?".* Trent replies, *"I know that Callie is mad at me but if she has betrayed me then..."* As they sneak backstage and wait for Sabrina; Liam gets a link and is shocked but before he can show it to Trent; Sabrina comes with Nate. Sabrina angrily says, *"what do you think you are doing here?".* Liam says, *"Boss, I think you should watch this."* Trent sees the conference video; drops the phone in anger and looks at Sabrina saying, *"who do you think you are? This war you have declared to not just me, but the entire Mafia cartels needs to end."* Sabrina says, *"are you in your right state of mind?*

*Do you know who I am! how dare you have the audacity to threaten
and intimidate me?".* Liam picks his phone and tries to turn it on;
Nate takes his phone and records the confrontation between Trent and
Sabrina. Trent gives a stern warning while Sabrina rolls her eyes and
says, *"if you think I will back down and be scared of you Trent Reeves.
You have another thing coming your way."* Trent says, *"don't think you will
keep my Angel away from me".*

Sabrina laughs coldly and says *"you are under the wrong impression
of me keeping her with me. I am her mother, and you are responsible for
betraying her with lies and secrets".* Trent holds Sabrina's collar; Nate
holds a gun in his hand and says, *"let madam go".* Liam holds Trent
back; Sabrina and Nate leave; they soon leave and return to the hotel as
Trent says, *"I need to find Callie and speak to her."* Liam says, *"Boss maybe
we need someone to go undercover."* As they think of a plan of what to do
next; back in Santorini; Hazel and Oliver are at the beach; Hazel was
making a sandcastle as Oliver captures Hazel and says, *"babes you look
smoking."* As Hazel's smile turns to sadness; Oliver comes and hugs her
as Hazel says, *"I just wish my best friend had her happiness."* Oliver says,
*"I am sure Callie will have her smile back soon. I am starving; let us get
some food."* Callie feels restless in her room; she comes out and decides
to take a walk down the beach.

As the sunset reflects on the sea; Callie looks at it thinking about
Trent and everything; meanwhile Hazel and Oliver are eating a nice
dinner and romancing as Oliver says, *"I love you, Haze."* Hazel kisses
Oliver and says, *"love you more."* Soon, Storm comes into Callie's room,
he is stunned to find her not there but a note, *'heading to the beach
back soon'.* Back on the beach, Callie stops, she slowly walks towards
the water; soon her foot gets stuck as the wave hits her; Storm comes
to the beach as he looks around, sees Callie and panics. Callie chokes
on the water while Storm comes and brings her out saying, *"firefly I
won't let anything happen to you."*; Callie loses consciousness as Storm
carries her to the hospital. A few moments later Oliver gets a call from

Storm and says, *"what?"*. Hazel asks, *"babes what happened?"*. Oliver says, *"I'll explain on the way."* Oliver leaves the money and heads out with Hazel to the hospital. As Storm awaits outside; Hazel and Oliver come; Hazel says, *"Holden what happened to Callie? How did she?"*. The doctor comes and says, *"the patient will be kept overnight; please come back tomorrow."* Hazel says, *"please doctor, she is my bestie, and I can't let anything happen to her"*. The doctor looks at the two guys asking, *"are you all family?"*. Storm says, *"I am her boyfriend."* Hazel is stunned while the doctor says, *"please come back tomorrow."* Storm looks at Hazel before Hazel can ask and says, *"if I didn't say I was her boyfriend, the doctor wouldn't have given me information."* Hazel worries as Oliver assures her that Callie will be fine.

Chapter 55

The next morning: Callie opens her eyes as she looks around and wonders, *'where am I?'.* As the doctor comes in; she says, *"Good morning! How are you feeling now?".* Callie sits up as she says, *"I feel better, can I leave?".* The doctor gets her results and says, *"everything looks good and remarkably, the baby and you are fine."* Callie was stunned saying, *"baby?".* Callie looked confused as she tried to explain, however the doctor asked her further questions. Callie knew what the answer would be; Callie looked sad as she thought of Trent when the doctor says, *"we would like to keep you in just for tonight to make sure you are fully ok."* Callie nods as the doctor was about to leave; she asks, *"doctor can I please request you to not tell this to anyone?".* The doctor nods and leaves while Callie lays back in bed; As the doctor comes out and sees Storm and Hazel waiting; Storm asks, *"doctor can I see Callie?".* The doctor nods and says, *"please let her rest."* Hazel says, *"I will see Callie in a moment."*

As Storm came in; Callie got up and he says, *"I was so worried for you firefly."* Hazel calls Oliver to update Callie's state. Sabrina comes running in and asks, *"how is my daughter?".* Hazel says, *"Sabrina, she is ok."* Sabrina says, *"I want to know what happened."* As Hazel says, *"let's get a quick coffee."* Meanwhile Callie looked at Storm with tears in her eyes; Storm wiped them and says, *"you know I will always be here for you."* Trent and Liam had a source that Callie was in the hospital; Liam was working on some papers; Liam worries and says, *"Boss we spent a lot of money."* Trent says, *"that doesn't matter, I just need to see and talk to Callie."* Trent holds Callie's photo frame and thinks, *'Angel I am coming to see you soon.'* As Hazel and Sabrina talk about Callie; Sabrina sees the doctor who says, *"Callie is a strong fighter. don't worry she is fine."* Storm gets some food for Callie as Sabrina and Hazel come into the room. Sabrina hugs Callie asking, *"my baby girl are you ok?".* Hazel hugs Callie and says, *"don't you ever disappear like that again bestie."* Callie cries while Sabrina wipes her tears and says, *"I love you mom."* As Storm comes back in with some food; Sabrina feeds Callie who says, *"being fed by a loved one is another feeling."* Sabrina senses that Callie and Storm need to have a private minute and heads out. As Callie talks to Storm about her feelings; Storm says, *"firefly I don't want to be your second choice or option, you know how I have always felt about you."* As Storm mentions Trent's name; Callie sighs saying, *"me and Trent have a connection and that isn't going to go away; not that now I am pregnant with his child."* Storm looked crushed and pained hearing Callie's words.

Callie looks at Storm's pained expression saying, *"there's so much I need to think about, should I tell Trent? What will I do?".* Storm gives some advice as Callie begins to feel sick and heads to the washroom; As Trent lands in Santorini at the airport; Liam gives him a plan and a mask with a doctor's uniform to enter. Trent comes into the hospital, grabs a clipboard, and walks down the corridor. Trent came into the room, he was shocked to see a familiar person as he said angrily, *"What are you doing here?".* Storm and Trent began to argue; Sabrina came back into the room holding Callie's clothes as she saw Trent; the anger in her eyes became red as she pushed Trent outside of Callie's room. As Trent was outside the room; Sabrina angrily says, *"how dare you to come here?".*

Chapter 56

T rent looks at Sabrina who has hurt and anger in her eyes; she says, *"I warned you to keep away from my daughter! You've given her enough pain."* Trent says, *"please I can't be away from Callie; she is my life, and I can't live without her."* Sabrina threatens Trent saying, *"you betrayed my trust, not just Callie. looking me in my eyes and telling me my daughter was dead; what sick monster does that?".* Trent says, *"I know I was selfish, and I made a mistake."* Sabrina laughs and says, *"MISTAKE??? my daughter needs to heal from all the hurt and pain you have given her."* Trent drops on his knees and begs Sabrina for a chance; Sabrina says *"you can't expect me to give you another chance; especially around Callie. She deserves better."* Trent says, *"my fate is with Callie, and no one can come between us."* Sabrina says, *"I will protect my daughter till my last breath, and you will never get her."* As Trent gets up; he says, *"Sabrina, I am walking away now, but this doesn't mean I will stop fighting for her!".* As Callie comes back from the washroom; she notices Storm has an angry expression asking, *"what happened Holden?".* Storm turns and replies, *"firefly, Trent came here."* Callie was worried and headed out of the room. Sabrina says, *"sweetie you should be resting."* Callie asks about Trent as Sabrina says, *"sweetie he won't bother you."* Callie asks, *"mom you remember the documents I gave you against Trent; is it too late to end it to make sure he isn't punished?".* Sabrina does not know how to answer while Callie's face is filled with pain and she says,

"I will try to do something." Sabrina brings her back as she rests; Trent comes outside to a garden, sits on the bench, and thinks of Callie. Later that evening as the stars come out in the garden; Trent looks in the sky. Callie comes out of her room, passes the garden, and comes out. Just then, Trent smells and feels a familiar presence and scent as he turns and sees Callie. Callie says, *"Trent"*; Trent says, *"Angel"*. Trent tries to come closer to Callie however she says, *"I don't want to talk to you."* As she turns to leave; Trent holds her hand and pulls Callie closer to him saying, *"Angel, give me a chance and hear me out."* Callie's anger came out while Trent mentions Storm who says, *"you have no right to be jealous anymore! you lost all your rights the moments you betrayed my trust."* As Trent holds her close saying, *"I will always be in your heart, just like you are in mine."*

Callie wanted to tell Trent her news; she closed her eyes and remembered the lies and secrets that broke their relationship. Callie steps back and says, *"what you feel doesn't matter Trent! You hurt me in the worst possible way. Lying to my face about my mom; what is a relationship if there is no trust?"*. Trent has sadness in his eyes and asks, *"Angel can you really not give me another chance? Do you hate me that much to move on to someone else?"*. Callie looks sadly at Trent and says, *"it might take months or days for my heart to heal but right now; I want to be left alone."* Trent speaks of love; Callie snaps at him and says, *"don't you mention love Trent Reeves!"*. As they looked at each other and the night starry sky above them; Callie came back inside without turning back as she stroked her stomach. Meanwhile back in Italy, Kevin was in his office with his dad discussing a plan as a knock on the door interrupted them. Seth says, *"Son are you expecting anybody?"*.

Kevin nods and says, *"enter."* Nate enters and says, *"we need to talk."* Kevin says, *"dad I will handle this."* Seth leaves as Nate closes the door; Alayna sees Seth listening in and says, *"it's not good manners to eavesdrop"*. Seth rolls his eyes while Alayna says, *"let's go and do something."* Seth leaves with Alayna while Nate checks the coast is clear and reports back to Kevin.

Chapter 57

A s Kevin got impatient and says, "*Nate we need to bring our plan closer.*" Nate and Kevin discuss some ideas of what to do next. Kevin asks, "*is it possible to add a bomb into the PM car?*". Nate nods however he says, "*Sabrina is doing an excellent job of keeping Trent away from Callie.*" As they discuss a plan to arrange a meeting; Nate makes some notes as Kevin says, "*Nate don't forget to make sure that everything goes to plan!*". Nate says, "*actually I might have forgotten to mention about a recording I filmed when Trent met with Sabrina after the conference.*" As Nate leaves, Alayna comes in and says, "*there's someone waiting for you in the living room.*" Kevin comes to the living room; he is surprised to find an elder lady in a black robe. Kevin asks, "*your Honour what a pleasure for you to come to my home.*" Amelia says, "*I remembered your conversation regarding PM Anderson.*" Kevin acts sympathetic and concerned saying, "*I have a strong feeling that the PM is in danger.*"

Amelia asks for some more information, makes notes and then Kevin plays the video of Trent and Sabrina. Amelia is shocked and says, "*please forward me this video!*". Kevin nods as he sees Amelia out; he smirks evilly and thinks, '*Trent Reeves your destruction starts in 48 hours.*' The next morning back at the hospital; Callie is feeling much better and cannot wait to go home; As the doctor comes in asking, "*how are you feeling?*". Callie replies, "*better I think, thanks for the medicines.*" The doctor says, "*please don't thank me, it's my job to take care of others.*" Callie asks about her baby; she smiles as she gets the all-clear, rubs her stomach and says, *"you're my little dumpling."* As the doctor is about to leave; Callie asks, *"how long will it be until I find out the gender?"*. The doctor checks her schedule before replying, *"four weeks' time."* Callie rubs her stomach as she gets a glass of water when Storm enters and watches her. Callie says, *"Holden what are you doing?"*. Storm compliments her and says, *"I have been given orders from your mother to pick you up."* Callie says, *"including my little dumpling."* Holden laughs and asks, *"is that the name of your baby?"*. Callie rolls her eyes and says, *"you wouldn't understand; let's go."* On the ride back, Callie could not help but think of Trent and prayed that her mother had dealt with the matter safely. Meanwhile, in a courtroom, Amelia was with the other barristers and clerks in relation to Trent Reeves case. As the case concluded; Amelia came out and got a call from Sabrina. Sabrina says, *"Your Honour, I wish to speak to you on an urgent matter."* Amelia asks, *"what matter would that be?"*. Sabrina replies, *"regarding Trent Reeves; the documents that were brought in. I was wondering if the case can be..."* Amelia asks, *"have you been blackmailed or intimated by Trent Reeves?"*. Sabrina replies, *"no"*, however Amelia gives the final decision and says, *"I am sorry to inform you that the case concluded against Trent Reeves and a permit has been sent for his capture and arrest."*

Sabrina was shocked despite her attempts to try and resolve the situation. Amelia says, *"I wish you all the best."* Elsewhere Callie reaches home; Hazel hugs her and they catch-up. Storm prepares a delicious meal for Callie; Hazel says, *"I missed you so much."* Hazel notices the awkwardness between Storm and Callie saying, *"I can see you two have some stuff to talk about. I am going to go and check on Oliver."* As Storm puts the food down; Callie says, *"I never thanked you enough for helping me."* Storm says, *"firefly I do this all because I want to, and you know..."*. Callie says, *"I can never love you Holden because I've told you this many times, I love Trent and of course my little dumpling."* Storm hugs Callie and assures her that he will always be there for her. Callie feels warmth in Storm but also feels his sadness too; Callie's phone beeps, she checks and says, *"a message with a link."* Callie watches the video; she drops the phone in shock; Storm asks, *"firefly are you ok?"*. Callie sits on the couch replying, "NOOOOO Trent he.. my mom....". Storm makes her drink water just as Hazel comes back. Storm watches the video and says, *"Hazel look after Callie, I will be back soon."*

Chapter 58

As Storm leaves, Hazel comes over to Callie who is crying uncontrollably as Hazel asks, *"what happened?"*. Callie explains to Hazel what she did and replies, *"I wanted to get back at him"*. Hazel watches the video as Callie angrily says, *"if Trent lays one finger on my mom..."*; Hazel feeds Callie as she hugs her best friend assuring her that everything will be ok. Meanwhile, Trent is drinking in a hotel suite as he remembers Callie's cold words; Liam comes in and says, *"Boss there's something you need to see."* At first Trent is broken and ignores however Liam shakes Trent and shows him the video on his phone as Trent's pain soon turns into anger; Liam says, *"Boss I will prepare everything to get back to Spain."* Trent smashes the glass in anger and says, *"I will not run like a coward."* Trent asks, *"LIAM WHO IS RESPONSIBLE FOR THIS!"*. Liam explains Callie's actions while Trent smashes more bottle in anger saying, *"my Angel would never betray me like this!"*; Liam says, *"a wounded tigress is the most dangerous Boss especially what you did to Callie!"*. Trent angrily says, *"I want to see her face; how could she destroy me like this!"*. Liam says, *"Boss there's danger outside."* Trent says, *"I don't care if I get caught, I want her to speak the truth."* Trent takes his phone, leaves in anger as Liam gets worried.

Back at Callie's place, Sabrina has come home as Callie hugs her mom asking, *"why is this happening?"*. Sabrina says, *"sweetie seeing you in this state hurts me. please don't cry."* Sabrina sees that Callie still loves and cares deeply for Trent despite everything, she says, *"sweetie I will see what I can do to help Trent escape."* Callie hugs her mom saying, *"mom what happens if Trent finds out that behind his capture is my hand?"*. Sabrina kisses Callie's forehead and promises to come back soon. Hazel comes to the living room as Sabrina says, *"look after my daughter."* Hazel nods while Callie says, *"mom don't go."* Callie holds Sabrina's hand; Sabrina cries as she turns back to Callie and has a small memory of a young girl holding her arm not letting her go. Sabrina embraces Callie and says, *"I promise no matter what happens, I will come back to you."* Callie lets her go while Hazel asks, *"Callie are you ok?"*. Callie felt her breathing tight as Hazel made her rest; Callie says, *"I feel like something horrible is about to happen."* Hazel says, *"your mom and Trent will both be ok."* As Trent came to the house; he banged angrily on the door and says, *"CALLIE, I KNOW YOU ARE IN THERE!"* Callie heard Trent's voice as Hazel checked through the window and saw Trent kicking the door in anger. Callie says, *"Haze; he's going hurt me."* Hazel says, *"don't worry, I won't let him get in."* Trent says, *"open the door; I don't believe you would betray me after everything."* Callie says, *"I don't want to see you, Trent; please leave."*

Callie was hurt and cried as Hazel hugged her friend. Trent bangs the door in anger and says, *"Angel, WHY DID YOU DO THIS TO ME? WAS IT PAYBACK? DESPITE EVERYTHING, YOU WERE THE ONE PERSON I LOVED MOST IN THIS WORLD!"*. Callie tries to apologize as Trent kicks the door in anger again and says, *"YOU HAVE MADE ME FALL SO DEEP! BE HAPPY THAT EVERYONE IS NOW LOOKING FOR ME FOR MY CRIMES!"*. Meanwhile, Nate is on the phone with Kevin who explains the plan as Nate says, *"it will be ready sir."* Kevin smirked evilly as Trent got a call and was stunned to hear it was Sabrina. Callie overheard the conversation as Trent stormed off as Hazel says, *"Callie what happened?"*. Callie takes her phone and tries to call her mom. Callie says, *"I need to call Holden maybe he can help."* Holden heard Callie's worries and assured her that everything would be ok. Meanwhile, Trent comes to a secluded location outside the city to the woods nearby a warehouse.

Chapter 59

As Trent awaits for Sabrina; he gets Liam's call who says, *"Boss I have prepared everything for our journey to escape."* Trent says, *"I have to see Sabrina, but I will see you as soon as I can."* Liam tries to raise his doubts for Trent who says, *"I have everything, under control."* As Liam packs a few more things; he hears a knock on the door, opens it and is stunned to see Storm. Liam thinks, *'what is the Storm doing here?'.* Meanwhile, Trent looks around; Sabrina walks towards him as he asks, *"why have you called this meeting?".* Sabrina replies, *"I want to help you escape to safety."* Trent laughs and says, *"you've changed your tune, why now?!".* Sabrina says, *"look I know you may think I despise you, but I know Callie still cares and loves you."* Trent says, *"yeah because selling me out to the world as a wanted criminal is such a lovely thing to do."*

Sabrina explains what happened with the proof; Trent rolls his eyes as Sabrina says, *"look just let me help you; for Callie's sake."* Trent looks at her coldly and says, *"I don't want your charity, pity or help to escape. I am fine to do this on my own."* Trent starts to walk away as he thinks of Callie when all of a sudden; a big explosion engulfs the forest as Trent is pushed to the floor; Trent turns back and runs to the scene. Trent was shocked to see fire and flames while Sabrina was on the floor; As Trent kneeled down and placed her head on his lap; Trent remembered losing Leone as Sabrina was injured badly while Trent says, *"you're going to be ok."* Sabrina begged, *"no hospital please."* Trent understood as Sabrina tries to make Trent promise to look after Callie. Trent says, *"Sabrina, Callie needs you."* Sabrina closes her eyes; Trent remembers everything he did to Callie and says *"Sabrina; you must be strong; I will make sure you keep every promise to Callie and get well."* As Trent calls Liam he says, *"alert the pilot to head to Italy. I'll meet you there."* Trent carries Sabrina in his arms and leaves; back in the house; a few hours had passed as Callie still had no response from her mom; as the doorbell rings. Callie opens, sees it is Storm and asks, *"did you get any news?"*.

Storm shakes his head as Callie worries for her mom; Hazel comes as Storm asks, *"firefly you need to not stress, why don't you get some sleep?"*. Hazel says, *"I'll prepare you a hot chocolate with marshmallows."* As Hazel makes Callie sleep; she comes and speaks with Storm who updates her on the situation. Meanwhile, a few hours in Italy in an abandoned warehouse near the docks Liam runs in to see Trent covered in blood asking, *"Boss explain what is happening? We should have left the country now."* Trent explains Sabrina's assassination as Liam asks, *"Is she dead?"*. Trent brings Liam to a room where Sabrina lays as the doctor is examining her. Trent says, *"danger is still around and that's why we need to make sure Sabrina gets well soon."* Trent says, *"when she was in my arms, it made me remember Leone and I don't want what happened to me to happen to Callie."* Liam says, *"Boss you still love her."* Trent nods as he asks the doctor for an update; Trent worries that Sabrina's condition may get worse as Trent angrily shouts at him. Liam asks, *"Boss what will you do next?"*.

As Liam heard his phone beeps as he gets a link and shows Trent the video in which news of Sabrina's assassination has gone into the media and Trent is declared the killer. Trent clenches his fist in anger and says, *"someone is out to get me! Whoever this person was they made a really good plan and to trap me!"*. Meanwhile back in Greece, Storm is smoking outside as he looks at the sea in thoughts when his phone rings. He answers as Rick says, *"Bud, check the link I have just sent you."* Storm watches and hears Sabrina's news as he is shocked. As he heads to check on Callie; she is still asleep as Storm thinks *'I can't let her know about Sabrina's death yet.'* Hazel brings Storm out of the room as she says, *"Oliver just called me to inform me to offer respect and commiserations to Sabrina."* Hazel asks, *"what is going Holden?"*; Holden tells Hazel the news of Sabrina's death and she too is shocked.

Chapter 60

Back in Italy, Liam was stunned to hear Trent's words who says, "*calm down Liam, I have a plan and I need to you listen very carefully.*" Liam nods as Trent explains Sabrina's final words before she closed her eyes; Liam nods and listened and says, "*Boss you are going to play into their hands.*" Trent nods and says, "*just as they expect me to.*"; Trent turns back to Sabrina, Liam asks, "*Boss what should we do if it takes months or weeks for Sabrina to awake?*". Trent turns back and replies, "*I will be giving myself up.*" Liam is stunned by Trent who explains what he intends to do; Liam says, "*Boss what about Callie? What if she finds out and hates you?*". Trent says, "*in her eyes, I will be known as the Fallen Angel, but this is the only way I can prove to her everything and keep my word.*" Trent says, "*the main thing is she will have her mother and even if I am not by her side, I know someone who will be.*"

As Liam sees Trent's sadness, he cannot help but feel his Boss's pain too; Back in Greece; Storm was in the living room in deep thoughts as Hazel came in asking, "*Holden does Callie know the truth about Sabrina?*". Storm shakes his head replying, "*Hazel, this all seems like a nightmare.*" As Callie awakes and comes to the living room, she is stunned to see Hazel and Storm in black outfits; Storm says, "*firefly there's something I need to tell you.*" Callie looks around and asks for her mom; camera flashes come through the window while Callie is confused; Hazel comes by her side and hugs her. Storm says, "*your mom has been murdered Callie.*" Callie laughs and says, "*Holden it's not good to joke about this."* Hazel tries to explain, Callie says, *"you too?"*. As Callie sees their serious expressions. She panics and says, *"Trent was the last person with my mom."* As she dials Trent's number he does not answer. Storm tries to calm Callie down however she says, *"I need to go to see it for myself."* Back in Italy, Liam told Boss about the police station however Trent says, *"we still need to go back to Santorini as I need to see Holden."* Liam and Trent boarded the plane as Trent thought of Callie and what she must be going through. As Storm and Callie come to the explosion area surrounded by flames and fires; Nate says, *"Callie you shouldn't be here."* Callie says, *"find my mom."*

Storm takes Callie from the smoke's safety. Callie cries in the car and says, *"Trent couldn't have hurt my mom. I know he has done a lot of things but..."* Callie cries and Storm tries to comfort her; he gets a call, answer it to Liam who asks to meet near the sea. Callie says, *"I can't believe my mom has gone. I know she is ok."* Callie screams as she begins to get pain in her stomach while Storm brings her home and calls the doctor. The doctor says, *"Callie has received a big shock, you will have to look after her, so she faces no more stress."* Storm nods as later that evening he says, *"Hazel, I need to go out for some business, take care of Callie."* Nate makes a phone call to Kevin to inform him that Sabrina is dead. Seth, Alayna, and Kevin toast and says, *"very soon Trent will be locked up."* As Storm came to the sea to meet Liam, he was stunned to see Trent as Storm ran over to him and asked him about Sabrina. Trent acts coldly and says, *"yes she was the last person with me but she's dead now!"*. As Storm grabs Trent's collar angrily, Callie awakes and remembers her mom's death. Callie does not believe Trent could do that as she opens her backdoor for some air and she sees Storm in the distance. She walks downstairs as Hazel comes back to the room and wonders, *'where did Callie go?'*. As Storm berates Trent for his actions. Trent angrily says, *"she shouldn't have declared an enmity against me! I am Trent Reeves and anyone who tries to betray or starts a war against me ends up dead! I killed Sabrina."* Callie sees Trent and Storm as she hears those three words,

'I killed Sabrina'. Callie says *"HOW DARE YOU!! TRENT WHY!!"*. Trent is stunned to see Callie who screams in anger and says, *"ALL I EVER DID WAS LOVE YOU AND YOU MURDERED MY MOM."* Callie faints as Storm runs over and holds her; Trent looked hurt and shocked to see Callie's state. As Trent was about to come over to Callie; Storm stops him and says, *"leave you don't deserve her love or anything!"*.

Chapter 61

Trent was hurt by Storm's words, and he left while Storm carried Callie back to her room. As Hazel called the doctor to check on Callie. Storm stroked Callie's forehead and says, *"firefly you will be ok."* Back in Italy, Kevin had a meeting with Amelia who says, *"without a body or proof how can we give Trent Reeves a sentence?".* Kevin thought, *'I must make sure Trent gives himself up.'* Back in Greece, the doctor examines Callie and says, *"I have told you; she must not face any stress."* Callie awakes with Hazel beside her, Hazel makes her drink water as Storm comes in to check on her as Callie says, *"Trent wasn't here, and he didn't say he murdered my mom."* Storm says, *"I am sorry firefly."* Callie wipes her tears and says, *"He didn't just kill my mom Holden, he has killed me and my love for him."* Callie says, *"I won't let Trent anywhere near my baby."* Storm was stunned by Callie's decision while she says, *"promise me both of you, you will never tell Trent."* As they look at each other and promise, Callie rubs her stomach and says, *"my baby will never know that their dad is a murderer."* As Hazel and Storm head out to talk, Callie speaks to her baby and says, *"my little dumpling mama is going to protect and love you."* As Hazel asks, *"Holden what happened? Why is Callie being so much pain over Trent?".* Storm tells Hazel about Trent and Callie's state. Hazel cannot believe it as she says, *"I would have never thought of Trent capable of murdering Callie's mom."* Storm says, *"Callie's condition is becoming serious."* He calls the doctor to arrange an ultrasound as Hazel comes and sits with Callie.

Meanwhile, Trent has come to Amsterdam in Callie's apartment as each corner is filled with her scent and memories. Trent grabs a bottle of whiskey as he calls Liam who updates him on Sabrina's state and says, "*Boss she is still in the same condition.*" Liam asks, "*did you speak with Holden?*". Trent tells Liam what happened as Trent asks, "*can you check if Callie is in the hospital?*". Trent says, "*it's just the way that Callie collapsed, and I feel it's more than just stress.*" As Liam asks, "*Boss where are you?*". Trent says, "*making one last stop at Callie's apartment before I give myself up.*" Liam tries to talk him out of it, Trent is firm as he drinks a last glass of whiskey and holds Callie's photo and says, "*I love you Angel.*" Trent says, "*Liam maybe fate doesn't want me to be with my Angel, but I want you to be the next leader of the Black Panther if something happens*". Liam says, "*Boss no I can't! why are you talking like this?*". Trent ends the call, comes back to the airport as the pilot asks, "*Boss where should I take you?*". Trent replies, "*Italy.*" As he is on the way to Italy a message beeps on his phone as Trent is shocked and angrily thinks, '*the person who tried to kill Sabrina is still out there.*' Trent promises that no one will harm Sabrina or Callie. A few moments later in the police station, two officers are speaking about Sabrina's murder. Trent walks in. he says, "*I didn't know gossip was so hot.*" The officers turned and were stunned as they bowed down in front of Trent. Trent did not know if they feared him or if they were respecting him.

Meanwhile, at a secluded location, Kevin and Seth were talking as Seth says, "*I have a plan son.*" Kevin says, "*what plan will work if Trent is not in prison? Looks like your text message to Trent to scare him did not work!*". Seth says "*I have my man, Vyom. He will kill and finish Trent in prison.*" As Seth further explains the plan, Kevin smirks evilly. As the two officers stand up, Trent says, "*I am here to give myself up!*". The next day back in Santorini; Callie was feeling nervous and worried over her appointment and says asks Storm, "*Holden what if something happens to my little dumpling?*". Storm reassures her and says, "*firefly you're a warrior and your baby will be a warrior too.*" As the doctor called them in, Callie lifted her top, laid on the bed as the doctor says, *"this might feel a little cold."*

Callie feels the coldness the doctor puts on the machine while Callie soon sees her baby on the screen. Storm holds Callie's hand asking, *"wow is that my little dumpling?"*. The doctor smiles as Callie asks about her baby's health. The doctor says, *"your baby is strong and healthy, would you like to know the gender?"*. Callie nods as the doctor replies, *"you're having a baby boy."* Callie was excited as Storm assured her that she will be the most amazing mother. Callie says, *"I have my son's named chosen, he will be called Trey."* A few hours later Hazel manages to finish packing as she finishes her call with Oliver. Callie comes back, see Hazel's bags packed as she says, *"Callie I need to head back to manage the bakery and Oliver is missing me."*

Hazel asks about Callie's appointment. Callie heads to the washroom as Storm says, *"Hazel, Callie is going to have a baby boy and she is feeling very emotional right now about Trent and everything."* Hazel asks, *"did Callie choose the name for her son?"*. Storm nods and replies, *"Trey."* As they talk, Storm's phone beeps as he opens the message which shows a link. Hazel notices Storm's worried expression as she watches the video; Kevin makes a statement about Sabrina's death and Trent's arrest. After watching the video, Hazel and Storm are both in shock after hearing Trent's prison sentence of forty years. Callie comes back, notices Storm and Hazel looking worried and asks, *"Is everything ok?"*. Storm tells Callie about Trent's arrest and sentencing however Callie's reaction is cold and says, *"this is what he deserves! He murdered my mom."* Callie comes back to her room to rest, she sits on her bed, looks in the mirror and wipes a tear from her eyes before stroking her stomach.

Chapter 62

Elsewhere, Liam was by Sabrina's side as he spoke to her trying to encourage her to get better and wake up. Liam says, "*Trent is doing everything in his power to protect you and Callie.*" Liam felt anger as he says, "*Boss is misunderstood despite everything that happened, he never wishes harm on anyone.*" The doctor comes in with an update and shows Liam footage of Trent sentencing to forty years leaving him shocked. Liam had many questions and thought, '*I need to speak to Boss.*' Liam told the doctor to look after Sabrina and keep him updated. The doctor nodded as Liam left; in the cell, Trent was pacing anxiously thinking of Callie and everything as soon an officer came to his cell and says, "*Trent you have a visitor.*" Trent sees Liam who asks, "*Boss how are you coping?*".

As Trent asks for an update on Sabrina's condition. Liam replies, "*it's still the same Boss.*" Liam shows Trent the footage of Kevin a press gloating about Trent's capture; Trent says, "*I still don't know who is this Kevin guy?*". Trent mentions the unknown text message, he gives orders to Liam to find out who is behind it. Trent says, "*I have a feeling that someone close to Sabrina has betrayed her.*" Liam is about to leave however Trent asks, "*Liam get in touch with Holden for me.*" Despite Liam's attempt to ask further into the matter, Trent is firmer to Liam and says, "*I am the Boss and I want you to follow my orders.*" Liam leaves, he makes a call to Storm however it goes to voicemail, and he leaves a message. Back in his office Alayna and Seth are talking about the plan as Vyom comes in asking, "*Boss you called for me?*". Seth says, "*you have been loyal to me all these years and now I need your assistance."* Vyom nods his head as Seth says, *"you will be given the ultimate honor of killing Trent Reeves."*

Vyom is stunned and shocked saying, *"Boss what do you mean? How do I do this when he is in jail?".* Seth said, *"Alayna explain."* Alayna explains further to the plan as Vyom is nervous and doubtful just as Seth threatens him, *"either you do the job or die!".* Vyom nods. Later that evening as Callie is asleep, Storm sees a missed call from Liam as he hears the voicemail. Storm catches a flight back to Italy and visits Trent. An officer comes to Trent's cell to inform him of a visitor, Trent comes to the visiting room and sees Storm. Storm looks at him coldly saying, *"I got Liam's voicemail that you needed to discuss something with me."* Storm feels that Trent is hiding something however Trent becomes cold to Storm. Storm mentions Callie and Trent clenches his fist in anger. Trent sighs and says, *"Holden, I want you to take care of my Angel, there are evil people out there wanting to hurt her, and I know you will be the best person to protect her, even if fate is against us. I want you to give her the happiness."* Storm was stunned by Trent's words as he mentions sacrifice and protection which makes Storm thinks there is more to the situation than Trent is letting on. As Trent soon heads back to his cell to sleep, Storm flies back to Santorini.

Seven months pass as Callie is heavily pregnant; she looks out the view from the balcony, Storm comes out and says, *"firefly I have prepared you some snacks."* Callie was in deep thoughts as Storm waved his hand. Callie apologized as Storm says, *"you look like you were miles away."* Callie rubs her stomach as she says, *"I will be holding my son very soon."* As Storm remembers Trent's word, he comes closer to Callie and says, *"firefly I want us to date."* Callie felt nervous while Storm spoke to her about his feelings. Callie thought about everything and said, *"Holden you have been by my side throughout these seven months, and I want to give us a try."* Holden kisses Callie as she hugs him. Callie says, *"there's one more thing I want to do. I want us to head back to*

Italy." Storm looked at Callie asking, *"are you sure?".* Callie nods as they soon prepare for the flight; Back in Italy, Liam comes to visit Trent and informs him of the source behind Sabrina's attack. Trent asks, *"who was it?".* Liam replies, *"Boss, it was Nate."* Trent refused to leave the jail and says, *"we need more proof; I want you to follow Nate and tap his calls and conversation. I am sure there is someone bigger behind the operation".* Liam nods as he soon leaves while Trent comes back to his cell and thinks of Callie. Callie is in the plane relaxing as Storm is also asleep; Callie stirs, takes Trent's photo out and thinks, *'seven months have passed but you have been in my thoughts.'* As they soon land back in a hotel; Storm takes care of Callie but soon gets a phone call from Oliver. Callie sneaks out, comes to the police station, takes a deep breath, and comes to the reception area. She says, *"I would like to meet Trent Reeves."* As Callie waits in the visiting room, Trent is stunned when he sees Callie with a huge bump. Meanwhile, Storm comes back into the room to check on Callie, he is stunned to find that she is not around and wonders, *'where could Callie have gone?'.*

Chapter 63

T rent was in shock seeing Callie with a baby bump, he felt speechless while Callie asks, *"what's the matter Mr. Reeves? Lost for words?"*. Trent replies, *"this is unexpected Angel... I never thought I would see you again."* Trent asks about Callie's pregnancy, Callie is cold and says, *"do not call me Angel you lost that right when you murdered my mother and for your information, this baby is not yours."* Trent was in a sad state, Callie could feel his pain, but she knew she needed to be strong and not fall weak. As Trent pleads and says, *"even if there is a small chance that baby could be mine..."* Callie coldly says, *"I have told you Trent that the baby isn't yours, but as you are determined to find out who it is? It's Holden and we are together."* Trent looks at her saying, *"there must be a reason you are here after so many months Callie".* Callie replies, *"I know what the media said and why you are here, but my heart doesn't believe you could have taken my mother away like that."* Trent says, *"all of this doesn't matter."* Callie felt anger and rage as she left the room while Trent watched her leave and his heart felt broken and pained.

As Callie came outside, she was stunned to see Storm waiting for her. Callie ran to Storm as he asks, *"what were you doing here firefly? How could you just disappear like that?"*. Callie had tears in her eyes replying, *"in all these seven months I thought my heart would have been right in telling me that Trent wasn't responsible for my mom's murder, but he didn't even give an explanation."* Storm brings her to a café as Callie says, *"I told Trent that the baby wasn't his."* Storm tried to get Callie to clear the doubts and confusion, Callie became cold saying, *"would you tell your child that their father murdered their grandparent? Trey will never know about this about his father."* As Callie cried, Storm comforted her and says, *"firefly I am sorry to have put you on the spot like that but if this is what you wish to keep Trey away from Trent. I will support you as always."* Later on, in the cell as Trent is speaking with the fellow inmates about Callie; Vyom comes in and says, *"Trent Reeves fallen leader of Black Panther."* Trent turns around to see Vyom who introduces himself as Trent is stunned to hear about what has been happening outside for many months. Vyom says, *"guess a whore broke your heart."* Trent's anger came to rage as he punched and kicked Vyom; he angrily says, *"DON'T YOU EVER SPEAK ABOUT CALLIE LIKE THAT EVER!"*. Vyom was in a bad state he headed back to his cell; Trent came to the payphone and called Liam who was beside Sabrina. Trent says, *"Liam I want you to come and meet me now!"*.

Liam rushed over to the prison to meet Trent. Trent had many questions to ask not just about his status in the Mafia but also about Callie. Liam says, *"Boss I am sorry I didn't know how to tell you."* Liam hands a paper to Trent regarding Callie's pregnancy he is shocked to see, *'Father's name is Holden'.* Trent scrunches the paper in anger and says, *"Liam once Sabrina is better, I don't want to nothing to do with Callie anymore!"*. Trent angrily storms back to his cell Liam leaves. Soon on the way, Liam heads back to see Sabrina who is still unconscious. Liam asks angrily, *"why did Callie have to hurt Trent like that? Destroying and breaking his heart?"*. The doctor comes in as Liam goes outside for a moment while Sabrina moves her fingers; the doctor notices Sabrina who opens her eyes.

As the doctor calls Liam back immediately, he runs in and sees Sabrina who is awake. Meanwhile, Storm asks, *"firefly are you sure you want to still stay in Italy?"*. Callie replies, *"you're right there are too many memories here."* Storm arranges for a car as they drive back to Amsterdam. In a private corridor, Vyom is speaking with Alayna about the failed plan of killing Trent. Alayna asks, "*how hard is it to kill one man?*" Seth takes the call, speaks with Vyom, and says, "*do you have any idea what is at stake?*". Vyom asks, "*how about a poisonous venom?*". Alayna and Seth talk nod, and Seth says, "*your work will be done in two days.*" Meanwhile Liam was by Sabrina's side as the doctor examined her. Liam asks, "*how is everything? why is she not talking?*". The doctor decided to run some more tests as Liam spoke to Sabrina who just kept blinking however in her mind, she had so many thoughts. The doctor comes back in saying, "*Sabrina you have just woken up from a seven-month coma. If you can understand anything around, you please give a sign either by your fingers or try to speak.*" Liam asks the doctor more questions, the doctor takes him to the corner and says, "*Liam she has just woken from a coma and patients especially in this state take time to recover, I will have to teach her how to talk and walk again.*" Liam says, "*this can't take much time; Sabrina is the key to helping the investigation*". As the doctor heads out to bring some medicines. Liam comes over to Sabrina who looks at Liam as he says a lot of things about Trent and what had been happening for so many months. Sabrina thinks a lot about Callie's and Trent's relationship saying weakly, "*C...C...*". Liam says, "*you are trying to ask about Callie, you want to know about your daughter right?*". Sabrina blinks as Liam tells Sabrina about Callie's pregnancy as a tear fell from Sabrina's eye. Liam understood Sabrina's emotions and feeling and assures her that she will get better soon.

Chapter 64

Trent was in his cell feeling anger over what Vyom had said about Callie. Trent had many deep emotions and thought as he punched the walls in anger making his knuckles bleed. Trent was still in pain after hearing Callie mention her relationship and baby with Storm. As Liam left the doctor to take care of Sabrina, he received an update from one of his men. Liam rushed immediately to the prison as Trent was called into the visiting room. Trent was stunned to see him while Liam says, *"Boss there's going to be an attack on you tomorrow."* Trent asks, *"what do you mean? I dealt with the rat Vyom here."* Liam replies, *"it's much more than that, Seth Romano is behind this."*

Trent's anger raged as Liam tells everything about the poison while Trent thinks and says, *"I have a plan Liam, you need to switch the poison with something else."* Liam was doubtful as Trent rolled his eyes and says, *"look this is a big trust on you for my life."* As Liam thought and says, *"I will speak with the doctor."* Trent asks, *"speaking of doctors? How is Sabrina doing?"*. Liam give the good news as Trent says, *"that's fantastic"*. However, Liam mentions further Sabrina's treatment and response, but Trent says, *"I have full faith that she will recover."* Liam says, *"one more time boss, you want me to switch the poison so you will die."* Trent sighs and whispers, *"look I will not be dead but merely faking it to escape."* Liam nods as Trent says, *"you can't tell anyone about this plan ok."* Liam nods and replies, *"yes Boss."* Meanwhile, but in Amsterdam in

Callie's apartment thing had changed as Callie had decorated the spare room into Trey's room filled with blue and toys.

Storm came in, saw Callie sleeping on the sofa and heard her speak of Trent. Storm's heart was broken as he says, *"firefly."* Callie awoke, saw Storm, and asks, *"is everything ok Holden? I must have fallen asleep for a long time."* Storm was cold towards Callie and says, *"despite everything in these last few months being by your side, it looks like you will never feel for me what I feel for you."* Callie was stunned by his words and says, *Holden, I am sorry for everything."* Storm snapped as he did not want any pity love, or care as Storm says, *"firefly I wish I could have been an important part of your life."* Callie says, *"you are an important part of my life Holden and the baby's too."* Storm walks out of the room and leaves the house. Callie begins to get pain as the door opens while Callie says, *"Holden??"*. As the person comes into her room Callie is stunned to see it is Hazel; Hazel calls an ambulance. A few hours later, Callie is being checked on by the doctor; Hazel is waiting outside as Storm comes and Hazel asks, *"how could you leave Callie alone like that?"*. Storm feels guilty the doctor comes and says, *"don't worry your friend is ok."* Hazel asks, *"are you sure?"*.

The doctor nods as Hazel heads into the room to see Callie. They share a hug as Callie says, *"I feel so heavy."* Hazel nods and says, *"yeah it's the pregnancy."* Callie notices a ring on Hazel's finger she blushes as Storm comes in asking, *"firefly can we talk please?"*. Hazel leaves while Storm apologizes as Callie says, *"Holden I don't want our friendship to be ruined because of your feelings for me."* Callie mentions her fears and doubt of not being able to give her son the best family and feeling of love. Storm holds her hand and says, *"never let your fear of doing something hold you back. You are never alone."* As Hazel comes back in and says, *"we should do something, how about ice cream for my bestie and my little nephew?"*. Five weeks pass, back in Italy as Sabrina has been receiving treatment to slowly speak again and has also been able to stand and walk slowly. Liam has been supporting her along with the doctor as Sabrina takes a walk down the corridor leaving the doctor and Liam to talk. The doctor says, "*I can sense that Sabrina is feeling emotionally pained possibly due to being without her daughter.*" Liam says, "*her recovery is going very well however in regard to bringing Callie; not right now.*" As Liam and the doctor talk about Trent's plan and mission, the doctor assures that everything will be done safely and without any complications for tomorrow. The next day early that morning Vyom speaks with Seth and Alayna about the plan.

Seth sees Kevin who wishes him luck and says, "*I can't wait to hear the news of Trent's death.*" Trent came out of his room he thought of Liam and the plan praying that things go well. As Trent comes to the canteen the chef gives him a special pasta and juice which he eats and soon begins to cough, struggle to breathe and collapses. The staff call for an emergency doctor as Trent lays on the floor. Elsewhere Callie comes to the park, sits on the grass, and looks around to see the trees and flowers blooming; she thinks of everything and talks with her baby. Hazel comes and sits with her as Callie asks, "*you still haven't told me about you and Oliver getting married?*". Hazel replies, "*I know so much has happened but he's my soulmate and I hope soon we will start our own family.*" As Hazel notices Callie is in deep thoughts, she asks, "*have you told Trent about the baby?*". Callie speaks to her son asking, "*Trey do you want me to tell you about daddy?*". The baby kicks as Callie says, "*I guess it's time to tell Trent the truth.*" Hazel says, "*I will drive you down there.*"

Elsewhere, Storm was hanging out with Rick and Oliver as they had lots of drinks and catch-up. As they reached the police station, Callie felt a little doubtful as Hazel asks, "*do you want me to come with you?*". Callie took her hand replying, "*I will be fine.*" Callie walks in, she remembers her last visit in the waiting room. As the door opened Callie felt nervous as an officer came out and says, "*you are here to see Trent Reeves?*". Callie nods as the officer tries to explain however Callie is persistent and says, "*I will come in there and see him myself if you don't let me meet him!*". The officer breaks the news of Trent's death as

Callie screams, "*NO!*". Hazel comes in as Callie's water breaks while Hazel says, "*you stupid officer! Call an ambulance.*" Hazel says, "*Callie it will be ok.*" The ambulance takes Callie away while Hazel calls Oliver and Storm to the hospital. Meanwhile, on the live news, Trent's death is declared as Alayna, Seth, and Vyom raise a toast in the victory of eliminating Trent.

Chapter 65

Callie is brought to the hospital she panics and screams feeling overwhelmed as Hazel tries to calm her down. Callie says, "*I can't do this Haze*". Hazel says, *"doctor please help my best friend she is in pain."* Callie says, *"Trent I need to..."* The doctor says, *"you need to breathe and give birth."* As Callie lays on the bed Hazel holds her hand. Callie squeezes as Hazel says, "*Callie you are hurting me.*" Callie screams and asks, "*why don't you try being in my position? I AM MORE HURT THAN YOU ARE RIGHT NOW!*". Storm and Oliver rush outside the room. Hazel says, *"I will be back in a second bestie."* Storm sees Hazel asking, *"how is Callie doing? What happened?"*. Hazel says, *"I will explain later but you need to come in now."* Callie was screaming and crying as Storm came in as Callie says, *"Holden help me."* The doctor comes back with more nurses and tells Storm to leave as Callie screams and Hazel holds her best friend's hand and gives her support. Callie says, "*I can't do this.*" Hazel says, *"you can, I've got you."* Meanwhile in a secluded location Trent is speaking with Liam as Trent says, "*Liam you are my brother, and I cannot believe you added laxatives into my food.*"

Liam gets emotional as Trent cocks his gun and says, *"if you ever do this to me again then..."* Liam gives Trent some clothes he changes. Liam updates him on what has been happening and says, "*Boss you have now officially been declared dead.*" Trent wanted to know about Nate and Kevin as Liam shakes his head and says, *"no update yet Boss."* Liam mentioned Callie's name, Trent felt a coldness and pain asking, *"why should she be bothered or concerned about my death?"*. Liam knew that Trent was still hurting after finding out about Callie and Storm's relationship. Trent asked, *"how is Sabrina's condition? Is she close to getting better? What is the update?"*. Liam shows Trent some of Sabrina's recovery videos however as Liam mentions, *"the doctor says that Sabrina can recover faster if Callie is by her side."* Trent shakes his head and says, *"We still need to find proof before this."* Trent handed a document to Liam who read it and says, *"Boss I can't do this!"*. Trent nods and says, *"you can, and you will be the new leader of the Black Panther!"*. Trent remembers Leone he closes his eyes for a moment as Liam signs the document asking, *"what is your next step Boss?"*. Trent formulate a plan as he says, *"once everything has been resolved I will be leaving."* Liam asks, *"Boss where are you going? I want to come with you."* Trent remembers Leone speaking of a special place in China as Liam says, *"you can go to any place in the world."* Trent replies, *"I need to heal everything, all my pain, and suffering."* Liam hugs Trent as Trent cries and Liam says, *"Bro you know I will always be here for you."* Trent says, *"you calling me Bro feels nice."* However, as they both stopped hugging. Trent says, *"I don't want people to think of me as a weakling."* Back in the hospital Callie was almost finished delivering her baby as Hazel says, *"come one bestie, you can do it for Trey!"*.

Soon, Callie relaxes hearing the baby's cry as the doctor says, *"congratulation on your baby boy."* As they take the baby to get a wash and cleaned up. Hazel says, *"bestie you did it."* Callie was crying as Hazel says, *"I will go let Holden and Oliver know."* Hazel sees Oliver and Storm waiting she tells them everything as Storm was stunned and shocked saying, *"poor firefly I can't believe that Trent is dead."* Hazel says, *"Callie will need us now more than ever."* As the doctor brings the baby to Callie she holds him. Callie sees Trey's eyes and says, *"you look so much like your daddy."* The baby smiles as Callie cuddles Trey and says, *"Mummy is going to love and protect you."* Callie thinks of Trent just as Hazel, Oliver, and Storm come in. Hazel holds Trey and says, *"aww my little nephew."*

As Oliver and Hazel give Callie a moment to speak with Storm. Hazel carries the baby outside while Storm says, *"Hazel told me what happened firefly."* Callie cries asking, *"why is fate so cruel to me? first my mom and now Trent?".* Storm hugs Callie and comforts her as Hazel brings Trey back to Callie. Callie looks at Trey as she sees Hazel, Storm, and Oliver watching her as Callie says, *"Trey these are your family and mine. Hazel is your aunt and Oliver, and Holden are both your uncles."* Storm holds Trey as he sees the resemblance of Trent however as the baby smiles he says, *"firefly he has your smile."* Back in Italy, Nate was on the phone with Kevin about the plan. Kevin saw on the TV and news about Trent's death. Kevin took out a toast of champagne as Nate felt guilty and Kevin threatened him. Elsewhere Trent and Liam overheard the conversation as they planned to expose Kevin and Nate. Liam made a call to one of his men and tracked Nate's home a young woman named Alice who opened the door, as a little girl ran to her mom. The man pointed a gun and said, *"get your husband and warn him if he tries to double-cross or tell anyone about the PM murder with Kevin Romano then you will suffer a fate worse than death".* Alice nods as the guy leaves while little girl asks, *"mama are you ok?".* Soon Nate opens the door and says, *"babes how are you?",* Alice asks firmly, *"Nate tell me the truth about Sabrina's murder!".* Nate was stunned as he confessed everything to her, and she felt sick. Nate says, *"babes you and Kelly mean the world to me."* Alice threatened to leave Nate if he does not make things right. Alice went to go and check on Kelly while Nate thinks, *'there's only one person who can help me.'* As he makes a quick call he leaves a voicemail as the doorbell rings. Nate opens the door as Liam walks in. Liam says, *"we need to talk."* As Nate answers coldly, Liam and Nate both argue as however Liam sighs saying," *look I understand you might be facing pressure from your boss! I am here to help you out."* Nate listened to Liam of who has a plan.

Alice came back in the living room, looks at Nate and says, *"this might be the only way to clear your guilty conscience."* Nate cries and Alice hugs him; Liam says, *"I will assure you that no one will hurt or attack your family."* Nate nods asking, *"what do you need me to do?"*. Liam replies, *"a worldwide broadcast this evening to clear Trent's name and identify the true criminals."* Meanwhile back in Amsterdam, Callie had finished feeding Trey and soon put him down to sleep. Hazel came into the room. Callie asks, *"Hazel what are you doing here?"*. Hazel replies, *"do I need a reason to come and see my favorite nephew?"*. Callie felt tired however did not want to leave Trey while Hazel says, *"I will watch Trey and you get some sleep."* Trey cries Hazel picks, him up and sings him a lullaby. Callie comes out of the room to see Oliver carrying a box; Storm sees Callie. She says, *"Holden, you know you are always welcome here to meet me or Trey."* Storm nods and says, *"of course firefly but I don't want to come between you and Trey."* Callie had doubts but Storm assured her she is doing an excellent job. Callie comes to her room she soon falls asleep. Back in Italy, Liam was speaking with Sabrina who had now fully recovered. Sabrina asked about Callie and Trent. Liam says, *"Sabrina you will see Callie soon however I am sorry to inform you that Trent passed away a few days ago."* Sabrina was stunned as she cries and blames herself however Liam assures her that Trent kept his word of keeping Callie and her safe. Liam tells about Nate and clearing Trent's name and exposing the real mastermind behind the assassination. Liam says, *"Sabrina I want to inform you that after tonight I will be flying back to Spain to manage the Mafia in Trent's memory."* Sabrina says, *"I only have one last question Liam about Trent's grave?"*.

Liam gives the address of a graveyard in Amsterdam and soon leaves. A few hours later Hazel comes to Callie's room; Callie awakes to wonder about Trey while Hazel says, *"there's someone here to meet you regarding Trent."* Callie comes to the living room and sees a man wearing a leather jacket he says, *"Good evening Miss Callie I will need you to come with me."* Callie had doubts however Hazel says, *"Callie you go, me and Oliver will watch Trey."* As they come out of the apartment and drive off. Callie gets worried as she looks around as they soon come out to the dockland in Italy. Callie asks, "*where am I? is this about Trent or my mom?*". The guy says, "*I am a member of the Black Panther Mafia.*" As they climb the stairs and soon come down a corridor, Callie feels a cold chill as the guy says, "*open this door and everything will be ok.*" Before he leaves he shows Callie a live broadcast which shows Nate confessing everything to Sabrina's murder. Callie is shocked to hear that Trent was not involved as she opens the door and sees her mom. Sabrina has tears in her eyes as Callie says, "*mom*". Callie has doubts as Sabrina says, "*touch me and feel me, sweetie, I am alive.*" Callie embraces her mom as Sabrina kisses Callie's cheeks and forehead and says, "*you've grown so much baby girl.*" Sabrina explains how Trent saved her; Callie cries in pain and says, "*how can I live with the fact that I despised and hated the man who saved you? I said so much to him mom.*" As Sabrina asks, "*Callie, are you and Holden together? And the baby too?*". Callie replies, "*Trey is Trent's son and when I look at him, he reminds me so much of him.*" Callie says, "*mom promise me you won't ever leave me again.*" She nods and they soon drive to Amsterdam while Callie tells her everything, they come to the apartment as Hazel is rocking Trey as Callie comes in with Sabrina. Hazel says, "*Ghost! Callie your mom's spirit is back to haunt us.*"

Callie takes Trey and gives her to Sabrina. Callie says, "*Hazel my mom's alive and there's so much to tell you.*" Sabrina speaks with Trey who coos happily however her phone rings, and she hands Trey to Callie; she says, "*I will be on my way.*" Callie says, "*mom, please be safe*". Sabrina kisses Trey and Callie before leaving to return to Italy. Meanwhile, Kevin is in anger over the news of Nate betrayal and speaks with Alayna and Seth. Alayna says, "*Boss we need to save ourselves.*" Seth ends the call just as Sabrina comes to the office; Kevin is shocked to see her and says, "*you can't be alive!*". Sabrina beats Kevin and soon calls the police officers to lock him up.

Chapter 66

Five years have passed, Trent has finished a training workout as he grabs his bottle of water. Po comes into the room as Trent asks, *"Master what are you doing here?"*. Po gives him the phone as Trent listens to the call and says, *"I will be on my way."* As Po worries for Trent, he bows and says, *"Po thank you for everything, I am ready to fly back to Amsterdam!"*. As Trent packs his bag, Po gives him a wrapped present with Po saying, *"you have been my best student and your father would have been so proud."* Trent hugs Po who says, *"we should have a farewell party."* As Trent checks the time for his flight and lets Po know; Po arranges for the party in Trent's honor.

Later that night on his flight Trent looks at a photo of Callie and thinks of her. The next day passes in Amsterdam as Callie comes to Trey's room and sees him still sleeping. As she opens the curtains and says, *"Trey rise and shine."* Trey pulls the blanket over him while Callie removes it, and she picks Trey up. Callie says, *"Dylan is waiting for you, and you know what today is?"*. Trey gets up excited and says, *"I can tell everyone my daddy is a warrior."* As Trey runs to the bathroom and gets dressed; Callie tidies up thinking, *'five years have passed and so much has changed. I still miss you Trent everyday.'* Callie gives Trey breakfast he is excited however he asks, *"mommy can we visit daddy later?"*. Callie was in thoughts as the doorbell ran; Callie opened in and a young boy ran in as Hazel says, *"hey Callie"*. Dylan and Trey ate breakfast while Hazel notices Callie is in deep thoughts and says, *"Oliver will drop the kids to school."* Trey comes back to his mom and ask about the answer to his question. Callie bends down and says, *"how about we see him on the weekend?"*. Oliver comes in and kisses Hazel he takes Trey and Dylan to school.

Callie and Hazel head to the bakery; Callie begins baking as Hazel says, *"every day I see Trey and he looks more and more like his father."* Callie cries as Hazel hugs her, Callie gets a call regarding an urgent order as Callie turns to Hazel asking, *"can you pick the kids after school?"*. Hazel nods while Callie leaves the bakery to go and deal with the urgent order, back in school Trey tells his class and teacher about his warrior dad. A few kids laugh at him and says, *"you haven't even got a dad. what a loser!"* Trey looks hurt and sad he sits back down; as Dylan says, *"don't let those bullies get to you".* Later that afternoon, business was busy in the bakery. Callie comes back as she sees Hazel dealing with work and looks at the clock and says, *"Hazel you need to go and pick the kids. Trey will be waiting."* Hazel grabs her bag and runs to the school; as Dylan is waiting and Trey is feeling bored he takes his football, walks down the road, and comes near a park. Trent is walking down the road as he comes to the park and looks at the flowers and trees thinking, *'everything here reminds me of my Angel.'* As Trey kicks the ball towards Trent he runs over to get and asks, *"sir you have my ball."* Trey looks at Trent who gives him the ball; Trent asks, *"little boy where is your mom and dad?"*. Trey replies, *"my mommy is working, and my dad is dead."* Trent looks sadly at Trey. Trent asks, *"what's your name, little boy?"*. He replies, *"I'm Trey, what about you?"*. Trent extends his hand and says, *"I am Trent."* As Trey explained how he came to the park, Trent asks, *"how about I drop you back?"*. In the school, Hazel was with Dylan, and they were looking for Trey. Trent walked Trey back to school, Trey asks, *"will I see you again? will you come see me the park tomorrow maybe? I want my mom to meet you".* Trent nodded and promised as Trey hugged Trent happily and went back to school. Elsewhere, Callie finished decorating her cupcakes and cookies she received a call informing her of Trey's disappearance.

Callie panicked and called her mother immediately. Trent came to his old penthouse as Liam was waiting for him and says, "*Boss I never imagined coming back here.*" Trent says, "*five years have passed, and everything has changed.*" As Trent told Liam about Trey he could not figure out why, but he felt a connection. Trent says, "*looking at the little boy he reminded me of my younger version, but his smile reminded me of my Angel.*" Trent looked at Callie's photo. Liam tells Trent about Callie's relationship as Trent looked at Liam for a few moments, but he says, "*wherever she is now, she must be happy.*" As Trent gets changed and Liam brings him to the basement. Liam comes in as Seth is locked up and Seth demands to be let go. Liam says, "*finally managed to track down a weasel like you.*" Seth says, "*if you uncuff my hand then you will see what I will do to you.*" Trent comes as Seth looks shocked to see him; Trent begins to beat and hurt him as Seth pleads and begs for another chance however Trent cock a gun and kills him. Back at school Hazel and Callie wait in the office as Trey opens the door Dylan says, "*Trey there you are.*" Callie hugs Trey and says, "*mom I'm sorry I left like that.*" Hazel says, "*Callie he's safe that's all that matters.*" Callie asks, "*Trey where did you go? I know Hazel was late to pick you and Dylan up.*" Trey talks about the trip to the park and mentions Trent's name, Callie feels fear and panic.

Hazel looks at Callie who looks in a shocking state and hands Callie some water. Trey says, "*mom you know me, and Trent made a promise to meet again.*" Callie's face changes to anger as she snaps at Trey who cries; Hazel takes him and Dylan home. Callie screams at the principal and says, "*HOW COULD YOU JUST LET MY SON WANDER FROM SCHOOL? WHAT IF SOMEONE HAD HURT HIM!*". Callie then left, came home as Hazel tries to calm her down. Callie snaps at Hazel and says, "*if you would have collected my son on time, nothing would have happened to him.*" Hazel says, "*Callie you are overreacting.*" Callie looked at Trent's photo as she told Hazel her doubts as the doorbell rang and Hazel opened as Sabrina ran in and asked, "*what happened to Trey?*".

Callie ran to her mom, hugged her as Sabrina could feel that Callie has been feeling worried and stressed. Callie told about Trey meeting with a guy in the park named Trent. Sabrina says, "*I will investigate this matter.*" Callie heads to the kitchen and makes a chocolate milkshake she says, "*I will speak with Trey.*" Meanwhile, Dylan and Trey talked, Trey cried and says, "*no one believes my daddy is a warrior, everyone was laughing at me and then mommy yelled at me.*" Callie came inside and says "*Dylan sweetie why don't you and see your mom? I need to speak to Trey.*" Callie put the milkshake on the table, sat on the bed as Trey says, "*I don't want to talk to you, mommy.*" Callie took Trey as he sat on her lap, and she apologized for shouting at him. Trey says, "*I am sure my new friend is not someone who will hurt me, mommy.*" Callie asked about the presentation at school while Trey cries and says, "*I wish daddy was alive, everyone was laughing at me.*" Callie wipes Trey's tears and hugs him. The next few days pass as Callie looks after Trey and makes sure he is safe; as Trent passes the park and thinks of Trey, Trent waits for hours as soon it gets dark and he leaves. Hazel and Callie were busy in the bakery as Callie comes and picks Trey from school however Trey says, "*mommy can we go see daddy?*". Callie nods and says, "*ok Trey but we will head to the park tomorrow?*". Trey says, "*really mommy?.*" He thinks, '*I hope Trent is there.*' As they come home Trey gets changed while Callie carries flowers and Trey holds a small warrior figure saying, "*I will put it on daddy's grave.*"

Chapter 67

C allie took Trey's hand and walked to the graveyard. Callie and Trey came to Trent's grave as Callie placed the white flowers on his grave; Trey says, *"daddy this is a special present for you"*. Callie cried as she spoke to Trent while Trey cries and told him about his presentation and his new friend and says, *"daddy you are my warrior and I forever love you."* Callie hugged Trey who says, *"mommy I love you."* Callie kisses Trey and says, *"I love you too Trey."* Hazel was with Oliver and Dylan while Oliver asks, *"is everything ok? babes are you worried about Callie?"*. Hazel kisses Oliver and calls Dylan over as she lifts her son up and says, *"you both are my world, you know that."* Oliver kisses Dylan and Hazel while Oliver says, *"I love you more and more each day."* The doorbell rings as Oliver opens to see Storm holding gifts; Dylan says, *"Uncle Holden."* Holden lifts Dylan who says, *"I've missed you so much."* As Storm hands Dylan the gift who runs to his room; Oliver and Hazel are surprised to see Storm as Oliver asks, *"bro what brings you back to Amsterdam?"*. Storm replies, *"what has been happening with Callie?"*.

Oliver goes to check on Dylan as Hazel prepares tea and tells Storm everything. A few hours later Hazel comes with Dylan to Callie's apartment as Sabrina opens the door and sees Storm. Dylan looks for Trey as Storm says, *"Sabrina, Hazel has told me about Trey's disappearance and meeting an unknown person."* Sabrina says, *"yes we don't know who he is, but he told Trey he was Trent"*. Later that evening

Callie comes in with Trey; as Storm sees Callie and says, *"hello firefly."* Callie was surprised to see Storm while Dylan says, *"you have finally come back."* Trey and Dylan play as Callie says, *"boys it almost your bedtime".* Hazel says, *"I will put them to bed."* Hazel reads the boys a story, Trey talks about Trent. Hazel says, *"Trey sweetie, I am sure your mom will meet your new friend soon."* Dylan says, *"I want to meet your new friend too, but he won't take my place as your best friend right?"* Trey shakes his head and says, *"Dylan you're my best friend in the entire world."* As Hazel manages to get the boys to sleep she comes out to see Callie. Callie hugs Hazel and apologizes for their fight a few days ago. Callie says, *"I don't want to see Trey get hurt or in danger."* Storm says, *"nothing will happen to Trey."* As everyone sits down to talk about everything. Trey stirs in his sleep and feels restless as he gets up to get a glass of water.

As he opens the door, hides behind the wall and listens. Sabrina says, *"Callie I think it would be safer if you and Trey head to Santorini for a few days whilst Holden and I try to figure out who this Trent person is?".* Callie says, *"I can't just leave Amsterdam, this place is not just mine but Trey's home."* Trey feels sad and says, *"I can't believe mommy doesn't want to meet my new friend."* The next morning as everyone is asleep, Trey gets changed; Dylan wakes up asking, *"where are you heading off so early in the morning buddy?".* Trey replies, *"mommy and everyone wants to take me away and I wants to see Trent".* Dylan asks, *"can I come?".* Trey replies, *"I will be back soon cover for me ok."* Dylan nods and heads back to sleep as Trey sneaks down the corridor and comes out of the back; he climbs the wall and runs. A few hours later after packing Callie comes into the room to get Trey however as she sees Dylan. Callie screams and Hazel comes in as Dylan wakes up asking, *"Auntie Callie why did you yell so loud?".*

Callie asks, *"where is Trey?".* Hazel looks at Dylan and says, *"answer Dylan where is he?".* Meanwhile, in the park, Trey sat in the flower field as he looked around to see it was quiet however he soon saw a familiar figure, got up and ran to Trent and hugged him. Trent says, *"Trey you're here."* Trey apologized as Trent says, *"I missed you seeing you."* Trey opens his bag, gives Trent a doughnut and also takes out a cupcake. Trent eats it and it tastes so familiar; Trey says, *"my mom is the best baker in the world."* Trent notices Trey is a little sad asking, *"what's the matter? Is your mom angry with you?"*. Trey nods replying, *"I left home without telling my mom."* Trent was shocked as he bends down and says, *"you shouldn't have done that, buddy."* Trey cries while Trent hugs him saying, *"I will inform your mom to come and pick you up."* Trey asks, *"what if she is mad with me?"*. Trent replies, *"how could a mom be angry with their child?"*. Elsewhere, Dylan tells everyone about Trey and his plan. Callie panics as Hazel says, *"calm down Callie I am sure Trey is safe."* Callie's phone rings Sabrina takes the call as Trent informs Trey is with him. Sabrina says, *"thank you."* After hearing the call, Callie gets Trey's location and immediately headed towards the park. As Callie runs down the path she sees under a tree Trey hugging the figure as the person's back is turned, Callie screams, *"TREY!"*. Trey runs to his mom who lifts him and hugs him; she says, *"I can't believe you left and ran away from home."* Trey apologizes and says, *"I only wanted to be with my friend."* Trent gets up, Callie asks, *"who are you? my son won't stop talking about you?"*.

Trent turns to face Callie, Callie puts Trey down and says, *"no you can't be real, you can't be my Trent."* Trent says, *"Angel"*. Sabrina comes, sees Trent and is shocked; Callie makes Trey leave with Sabrina. Trent looks at Callie as he comes forward however she steps back shaking her head and says, *"your grave... your death..."*. Trent says, *"Angel give me a chance to explain everything."* Trent says, *"I always wished you had happiness even if it was without me."* Trent asks, *"is Trey my son?"*. Callie nods, cries, and explains as Trent becomes angry saying, *"how could you do something like this Angel? Letting me think that our child was not mine."* Callie angrily points her finger and says, *"don't even try to accuse me of betraying you!"*. As they both argue with each other Callie says, *"I always told you lies, and secrets will break a relationship."* Callie came closer to Trent, touches his face and cries saying, *"you are really here in front of me?"*. Trent nods while Callie says, *"Trey is my life, please don't take him away from me."* Trent says, *"I've spent already five years apart from you and Trey and I want us to be together in our son's life."* Callie was stunned by his words; Trent says, *"Trey is our son's name."* Callie says, *"Trey Leone Reeves."* Trent was stunned and shocked to hear his son's full name as Callie explains, *"Trey is a combination of our names and Leone in memory of your dad"*. Callie wiped her tears, Trent pulled Callie into a hug as Callie embraced Trent who says, *"let's go home."* Trent takes Callie's hand she feels the warmth and a smile returning to her face.

Chapter 68

At home, Sabrina was with Trey who had lots of questions as Callie came home with Trent. Everyone was stunned to see him as Hazel slaps Trent asking, *"how could you do this to my best friend?"*. Oliver says, *"babes calm down."* As Sabrina comes out of the room; Dylan is speaking with Trey about everything. Trent says, *"I am glad that my Angel had her friends and family around her all these years."* Callie looks at her mom who says, *"you need to speak with Trey."* Trent was about to go; however, Sabrina says, *"you and I will have a chat."*

Trey looks at Callie saying, *"mommy there's something you are not telling me."* Callie sits with Trey and breaks the news about Trent. In the living room, Dylan comes to see Trent and asks, *"so you are Trey's new friend?"*. Trent extends his hand as Hazel says, *"Dylan."* Oliver says, *"babes I will take Dylan out for a small trip."* Trent says, *"Hazel I am happy that you and Oliver had your happy ever after."* Sabrina says *"don't try to change the subject Trent! Where were you for all these years?"*. After hearing Trent's side of the story Sabrina felt his pain and says, *"if you ever hurt my daughter or grandson ever again I will chop you up and feed you to the piranhas."* Trent laughs however soon worries when he hears a scream coming from Trey's room. Trent runs to the room and opens the door; Callie comes outside while Trent comes in. Sabrina says, *"Hazel put on the kettle."*

Trey sits on the bed as Trent comes closer saying, *"son."* Back in the living room, Sabrina is by Callie's side crying and tells her mom

165

everything. Sabrina says, *"sweetie you are not to blame for anything".* Hazel also assures her while Callie says, *"I need some air."* Trent was with Trey who says, *"mommy told me about you."* Trent says, *"son, I am your daddy."* Trey says, *"I always wish for my daddy to be with me."* Trent hugs Trey and says, *"son I will always be with you."* Trey says *"promise, daddy?"* Trent promises and they share another hug. Outside, Callie sat on the swing in thoughts, Storm came to see her as Callie explained everything to Storm. Trey came to the living room and happily saw everyone, Oliver came back with Dylan while Trey says, *"Dylan meet my daddy."* Trey says, *"I'd better say sorry to mommy."* As they head to the garden Trent saw Storm embracing Callie as he felt jealousy and anger built up inside. Trey calls out, *"mommy."* Callie embraced Trey as she says, *"my Trey."* Hazel comes out as she says, *"Callie the school has asked for Dylan and Trey to come back."* Trey says, *"I can't leave my mommy or daddy."* Trent asks, *"how about I drop you to school?".* Trey jumps and gets ready while Callie comes back in and sees her mom about to leave. Sabrina says, *"I will be back soon."*

Trey and Dylan come to school a few boys teased Trey however Trent warns them and says, *"don't ever mess with my son!".* Trey says, *"my daddy is the best."* Callie and Hazel are busy in the bakery as Callie feels overwhelmed, leaves early, and comes to the park. She sits under the tree thinks of Trent and cries. As the evening falls, she comes back to see Trent reading Trey a bedtime story as she comes into the garden. Trent find her, Callie is still crying; Trent says, *"Angel look at me".* Callie blames herself while Trent caresses her face lovingly and says, *"Angel you are never to blame for what happened."* Trent says, *"even all these years I spent apart from you, I never loved anyone else."* Trent pulls Callie closer; he kisses her tears as Callie looks at Trent who says, *"Angel be mine!".* Callie says, *"I am yours!".* Callie thanks Trent for everything as he asks, *"what do you mean?".* Callie replies, *"protecting my mom and giving me Trey."* Trent kisses Callie holds him close and passionately kisses him. Trent lifts her and carries her to her room where they make love. Callie says, *"Trent you will never leave me again."* Trent says, *"I will never my Angel for you are my life."*

The next morning Trent prepares breakfast as Trey eats it and says, *"this is the best pancakes ever!"*. Callie comes and kisses Trent, the doorbell rings; Trey opens to see Hazel and Dylan as they go to school. Callie says, *"I better get to work."* Trent says, *"I am sure we have time."* Trent lifts her on the counter and says, *"you're wearing my top Angel."* Trent feeds Callie the pancake she sexily adds the sticky syrup to Trent, as he lifts her and brings her to the bathroom; they make out and the shower soon becomes extremely hot. At school, the bullies apologize to Trey while Dylan says, *"this is good, and don't ever tease or bully anyone else."* Dylan asks, *"how are you coping with your dad?"*. Trey replies, *"he's amazing."* The next few weeks pass with Callie and Trent coming closer and rekindling their relationship, Trent has also managed to build a strong bond with Trey. He comes to meet Liam and says, *"I want to do something big for my son".*

Chapter 69

Seven months passed with Callie's business expanding worldwide as she was also having the best relationship with her love Trent. As she was in the kitchen finishing baking, someone came in as she turned around and said, *"Angel I thought we needed to go somewhere."* Callie felt a kick in her stomach as Trent rubs her stomach lovingly asking, *"is my little princess giving mommy a tough time?"*. Trent romances Callie who says, *"come on Trent we need to get to the hospital for my appointment."* As they came to the hospital and the doctor did an ultrasound. Callie had happy tears as Trent looked at the screen to see the baby growing. The doctor says, *"your baby girl is doing great."* Trent says, *"she is a strong princess like her mother."* Trent and Callie share a kiss as Callie says, *"we haven't really shared the news with anyone."* Trent asks, *"do you want to tell everyone?"*.

Callie nods as they soon come home; Callie comes to the garden as everyone yells, *"Surprise!"*. Sabrina hugs Callie and says, *"my beautiful daughter is becoming a mother again. you are making me feel so old."* Hazel says, *"I am so happy for my bestie."* As Trey comes over, Trent lifts him in his arms. Trey says, *"I can't believe I am going to be a big brother; I hope it's a boy."* Trent says, *"you're having a little sister."* Trey is still happy as everyone enjoys the party. Storm arrives and Trent talks and clear the misunderstandings, Trent says, *"thanks for taking care of my Angel."* Callie comes to Trent as they dance while Trent holds her; Callie says, *"I feel so big!"*. Trent says, *"Angel you are the most beautiful girl in the world and you're carrying our little princess."* Callie and Trent share a kiss as the fireworks explode happily in the sky with Dylan and Trey enjoying and laughing happily.

As time flies to Christmas, Trey is excited and says, *"this Christmas will be special because daddy is here."* Trent helps Trey to decorate and also put the presents under the tree. The doorbell rings as Sabrina comes in with gifts and so does everyone else. Hazel hugs Callie who says, *"I feel like our daughter will come anytime soon."* Hazel says, *"I have something to tell you."* Oliver and Hazel announce that they will be having their second child as Callie is happy for her friend. As Callie comes to the kitchen, Trent comes beside her as Callie says, *"this Christmas is really special because you're with me."* Trent wipes her tears and says, *"I don't want you to feel sad or cry, Angel."* Just then Callie feels a sharp pain as her water breaks. Trent asks, *"Angel are you ok?"*. Callie screams, *"OF COURSE I AM NOT OK! TAKE ME TO THE HOSPITAL NOW!"*. Storm watches Dylan and Trey as Callie is rushed to the hospital room as she screams and yells at Trent. Trent tries to calm her down as the doctor says, *"this is just like your first pregnancy."* Callie screams as Trent comes out of the room.

Hazel says, *"don't worry Trent, Callie was the same when she was giving birth to Trey".* Trent comes back into the room and holds Callie's hand. He supports her and says, *"Angel you can do this."* After eight long hours, Callie gives birth to her daughter as the daughter is taken away to be washed and is soon brought back. Trent holds his baby girl and says, *"Angel she looks like you, her eyes and nose."* Sabrina comes in with balloons with Callie saying, *"mom. You're here."* Sabrina asks, *"what have you named my granddaughter?"*. Callie looks at Trent who gives the baby to Sabrina replying, *"Hope".* Sabrina cries happily while Callie takes Hope and cuddles her. Trent and Callie share a kiss as Callie says, *"I feel so tired, but she is so beautiful."* A few days later Trent and Callie bring Hope home as Trey adores his little sister.

Trent makes a call he says, *"Angel I have some business to attend to and I won't be back for a few weeks."* Trent packs his bags, leaves while Callie misses him. Trent comes to a secret location in Italy and meets with Sabrina. Sabrina says, *"I can't believe that you are making me hide such a big secret from Callie."* Trent says, *"I had planned a Christmas proposal, but she gave birth to our daughter."* As the weeks pass it is New Year's Eve; Callie calls Hazel however she does not pick up. Callie cuddles Hope as she cries while Callie says, *"I know you are missing your daddy."* As Trey gives his mom a box gift, she comes to the living room and sees Hazel and Storm. Storm takes Hope while Hazel brings Callie to a room and dresses her up. Callie is made to wear a blindfold as she comes into a car. Callie worries as the car stops and she comes out. She removes her blindfold to see a beautiful town square decorated with lights and flower petals. It is empty as Callie sees herself in a white dress as she walks downs however someone holds her hand. Callie turns to see it is her mom; Sabrina says, *"my beautiful baby girl."* As they walk down the square the guests soon come out as Kaitlyn says, *"you're a beautiful bride Callie."* Daphne says, *"congratulations Callie."* Annabelle says, *"wishing you all the happiness."* Trent comes with Trey in matching tuxedos. Callie smiles as Trent says, *"Angel you look so beautiful."* As Trent takes Callie's hand the priest says, *"we have gathered here to join Callie and Trent in holy matrimony."* Callie looks at Trent as he says his vow, *"Angel so many years have been spent without you but not anymore, I love you and our kids. I want to be there always for you, be your best friend, your soulmate."* Callie says, *"Trent I love you so much, losing you broke me apart but now with you by my side, I cannot imagine a future without you and our kids. I choose to be yours always and forever."* As they exchanged the rings and both say, *'I do'*. They are both pronounced husband and wife as they share a kiss; Trent lifts her in his arms as confetti and rose petals fall above them. Storm comes with Hope who says, *"I think this call for a family photo."* As everyone gathers around the photographer captures the photo of Trent, Callie, and everyone. Trent and Callie share another kiss as Trent says, *"you're mine now forever Angel!"* Callie kisses Trent and says, *"I will always be yours."* They both say, *'I love you'* as their foreheads meet and look into each other eyes with love.

Chapter 70

Thirteen years have passed as Dylan and Trey have grown up now as teenagers. Hazel and Oliver have a daughter named Ariana while Oliver and Hazel were both more in love with each other; as Trey and Dylan were hanging out playing football. Dylan says, *"I can't believe thanksgiving is coming up soon."* Trey says, *"you're right buddy I can't wait."* Just then Trent came, as Trey says, *"hey dad what's up!"*. Trent says, *"come on Trey we have training."* Trey says, *"dad I don't really want to do this."* Trent says, *"son, your grandfather Leone passed the Black Panther to me when I was your age and soon you will be a great leader."* Trey sighs and says, *"Dylan I have to go."* As they come to a training field; Trey takes the gun and prepares to practice shooting. Meanwhile Callie is at home baking with Hope as she says, *"mom I love your chocolate and pineapple cookies."* Callie says, *"I am so happy you like it."* As the doorbell rings, Callie opens to see Hazel and Ariana; Hope says, *"Ari you're here?"*. Ariana and Hope shared a hug and headed into the kitchen while Hazel says, *"the girls are still hooked on your treats."* Callie laughs and heads to the kitchen as Ariana asks, *"Hope would you like to come with me to the concert tomorrow?"*. Callie gives permission the two girls dance however Hope says, *"I still need to get dad's permission."*

Callie says, *"leave that to me."* Trent and Trey soon head home; Trey heads upstairs to shower as Trent comes to the kitchen and says, *"hey Angel and everyone."* Hazel takes Ariana home while Hope tidies the kitchen. Callie comes with Trent to the living room and romances with

Trent. Trent asks, "*you are after something Angel?*" Callie says, "*Hope is going to a concert with Ariana tomorrow*". Trent comes and says, "*Hope you are not allowed to go to the concert*". Hope cries and runs upstairs as Callie says, "*really nice going Trent.*" Trey comes downstairs as Trent explains what happened with Trey saying, "*dad, Ariana and Hope have been planning this forever and come on Hope will be fine.*" Trent came upstairs Callie looks at him and says, "*you're sleeping on the couch.*" Trent knocks on the door as Hope opens and he comes in. As he talks with her and says, "*look you're my baby girl and I don't want anything bad to happen to you.*" Hope promises to be safe as she hugs her dad who happily gives her permission to go. Later that evening, Callie gives Trent a pillow, he throws it, pulls her close, and says, "*you think I am going to let go of my Angel*". Callie replies, "*you didn't make it up with Hope?*". Hope comes in and says, "*mom, dad said yes!*". Hope leaves her parents while Trent winks playfully at Callie as they share a passionate kiss.

The next few weeks goes by quickly as Hope, Hazel and Callie begin preparing for thanksgiving while Oliver makes calls and invites everyone. The day finally arrives as Callie decorates the table in the garden, finishes decorating the cake and preparing the biggest turkey. As the evening arrives Callie gets dressed in a blue sparkly dress, Trent wore a tuxedo as he pulls Callie and says, "*Angel you look sinfully tasty, I want to hold you and kiss you in ways you dream.*" Callie says, "*Trent that sounds so naughty and right now we need to manage to our family*". Callie blows a kiss to Trent as she heads down to open the door. Sabrina hugs Callie as she brings two presents and says, "*Trey and Hope my two favorite grandchildren.*" Hazel and her family come in as Dylan, Trey, Ariana, and Hope all hang out in the living room. Finally, Storm, Rick and Liam come with presents as Trent welcomes them. As they all sit outside and pray before they eat and dig in. Trent tries to romance with Callie under the table as Callie whispers, "*Trent stop*". Trent gets up and makes a toast to his family and friends while Callie smiles. Trent kisses

Callie as everyone says, "*get a room!*". They all laugh as later that evening after dessert everyone soon heads back home. Callie changes into her nightie in her room, Trent comes behind her, kisses her forehead, and says, "*you're my light forever Angel and I love you.*" Callie blushes and says, "*I love you more Trent Reeves.*" He lifts her in his arms and brings her to the bed as they make passionate love; Callie kisses Trent and says, "*you're my forever.*"